The Practice of Acknowledgments

How To Experience More Caring And Rewarding Relationships In Your Personal and Professional Life

Peter Anthony Gales

To request permission or for more information, please write to:
E-mail: pgales@thepracticeofyourlife.com
Website: www.thepracticeofyourlife.com
Facebook: www.facebook.com/peteranthonygales
Linkedin: www.linkedin.com/in/peteranthonygales
Twitter: PeterGales

ABOUT THE PRACTICE OF ACKNOWLEDGMENTS

"You have a lovely smile."
"You make a difference in my life."
"Dude, you messed up!"
"People this situation is costing us money."

These are all acknowledgments and this book explains how being acknowledged is a fundamental human need, and how giving effective acknowledgments is an essential business skill. A simple practice of acknowledging others can make a dramatic difference. Relationships can recharge and become more passionate, intimate, and playful. The workplace environment can become trusting, supportive, and less costly.

This book gives you the fundamental mechanics you must employ in your daily social interactions to have relationships where people feel safe and trusted enough for them to take initiative, and willingly receive direction and feedback without feeling threatened or taking things personally. It distinguishes the different forms of acknowledgements, including how to give them, and how to make a game of your practice at home and at work.

The Practice of Acknowledgements will teach you how to better observe people, their contributions and situations, and then show you how to let them know that you notice the difference they make—even when it's not good. Learning how to effectively acknowledge both the good and the bad actually improves the quality of your personal and professional relationships. A truly simple practice with dramatic benefits, *The Practice of Acknowledgements* can help any business professional or person seeking to create and maintain rich, rewarding personal relationships.

TABLE OF CONTENTS

Acknowledgments

I would like to acknowledge the work of Werner Erhard, and of all of the people who have continued it at Landmark Education.

I'd like to thank Patrice Matthews, and Greg Ifill, for taking the time to read the manuscript. Special thanks to Max Alvarez for his editing skills and contributions. Thanks to Chris Elliott, Robert Gedaliah, Bill Berg, Melissa Roberts, and my mother Pearle Phillips for contributing real life examples of acknowledgments. Thanks to Scott Hilton-Clarke for your unwavering support and for always being there for me.

To My Mother,

who is fond of saying,

"Kind words oft obtain what harsh ones fail to gain."

INTRODUCTION

The Life-Giving Words Of Acknowledgment

"Appreciation can make a day, even change a life. Your willingness to put it into words is all that is necessary."

—*Margaret Cousins*

One morning, I was standing in the elevator of my building and a woman came in with her children. We gave each other smiles of recognition, and then I resumed watching the passage of the numbers towards the ground floor. It couldn't have been more than two floors later when she said, "I've seen you around the building, and you seem like such a nice man."

"Wowww!" I said, truly blown away by the sincerity, warmth, and generosity of her words. "That's very nice of you to say."

"I mean it." She went on, "There is something special about the way you smile and look at people."

There was no agenda in her speaking to me except to acknowledge me for what she saw, and the effect was immense. I thanked her for sharing and left the elevator, walking to my destination feeling "Tony-the-Tiger **Grrreaaaaat!**" which lasted the rest of the day.

That acknowledgment played a big part in my writing this book.

I believe that if people regularly acknowledged each other, there would be a lot less anger and frustration in the world, and a whole lot more enthusiasm, passion, excitement, and willingness to help each other.

A world that works for everyone is built on trust, commitment, and acceptance of differences and what is. A practice of acknowledgment is necessary for these values to thrive. I've seen the difference small gestures make in building relationships, and the appreciation people feel for courageous acts of acknowledging mistakes and situations that don't work. Yet, as I look around, I see that most people not only do not have healthy practices of acknowledgment, they don't even have a distinct or conscious language for it.

I wrote this book to help every person create more trust and love in the world, to open up possibilities of new and stronger relationships in both our personal and business lives.

Relationships will prosper because they will be based on love, the kind of love that allows you and the people in your life to be just the way you each are, and are not. So many people would have more confidence and self-esteem if as children they felt that they were loved just for who they were, that they were loved no-matter-what.

The essence of acknowledgment is this same level of acceptance, and its foundation is love. Your Practice of Acknowledgment will allow you to express your recognition of the way things are in the world and in your relationships and thereby facilitate your acceptance of things that you may be resisting.

"What you resist persists."

—*Carl Jung*

Positive, lasting change comes when you genuinely accept how things are and are not, which immeasurably benefits your peace of mind and your ability to move forward in life.

Acknowledgment opens up communication between strangers and deepens relationships with existing friends and family members. *A genuine, heartfelt acknowledgment can build trust faster than years of delivering on commitments.* The minute you give the acknowledgment, the world changes. It becomes a better place. The longer you wait to give an acknowledgment is the longer you deprive everyone of a gift.

"A genuine, heartfelt acknowledgment can build trust faster than years of delivering on commitments."
—*Peter Anthony Gales*

To be sure, the practice of acknowledgments already exists as industry; specifically, the entire seven and a half billion-dollar greeting card industry, which is based on this practice[1]. Hallmark knows the emotional value we receive from acknowledgments and strives to have us acknowledge each other more. Earning a living through people's acknowledgment of love and friendship, and causing more of it—what a great business model!

Still, people often send cards out of obligation, rather than heartfelt acknowledgement. Perhaps this book will help more people see the meaning, relevance and value of acknowledgments in their lives. Through adopting a conscious practice of acknowledging people, you will find that it builds personal and business relationships, enriches your life and generally makes the world a better place.

Who Will Benefit From Reading This Book?

The practice of acknowledgments describes a fundamental mechanism of human social interaction, and therefore is relevant to every person who wants to be responsible for strong, healthy relationships in his or her life. At the core, we are social beings who cannot live—at least, live well—without other human beings in our lives. Developing a regular personal practice of acknowledging others can provide a healthy foundation for social interaction that enables the world to be a better place.

This book also has some very practical applications for the workplace. When operating at the core of any company culture, these basic principles can promote trust and yield greater willingness and ability of teammates to work together harmoniously and productively, thereby increasing performance and diminishing employee turnover and its associated costs.

How To Read This Book?

Read according to your own personal style, but I think it would be helpful to read *What an Acknowledgment is* and *the Key Characteristics of a Good Acknowledgment* first if you intend to jump around.

BENEFITS OF ACKNOWLEDGING

What An Acknowledgment Is And Is Not:

An acknowledgment is an authentic, sincere expression of the truth about a person or a situation. It is not offered in order to do or get anything, but rather as a selfless act to share the recognition of the truth about how something is or has been. An acknowledgment can be a supreme act of acceptance of what is—and is not—about a person or situation.

It is expressed in writing or speaking to the person being acknowledged. In cases where a situation is being acknowledged, it is expressed to the persons causing and/or affected by the situation.
In order to more clearly understand what an acknowledgment is, it is helpful to distinguish what an acknowledgment is not.
An acknowledgment is not:

Flattery; flattery is an overt use of insincere expressions of praise in an attempt to manipulate someone's opinions or actions.

A quid pro quo; acknowledgment is not done with an expectation of getting something in return, it is one of life's many mysteries that this simple act of giving yields such an immense reward. In other words, you will get something back, but only when it is given entirely as a gift to another.

The difference between an Acknowledgment and a Thank-You

A thank-you is an acknowledgment of an act, e.g. your holding the door, passing the salt, or getting me that job interview. Yet because society has very clear rules on how and when to say "thank you" for these *acts of doing*, a thank-you is also a quid pro quo and hence different from the acknowledgments that are the focus of this book. Thank-yous and apologies occupy a grey area because they are quid pro quos, however since they also recognize the existence of something or a situation, I include them as technical forms of acknowledgment in this book. Society has taught you how and when to give a thank-you or an apology; that's not the case with acknowledgments.

A thank-you is expected, while an acknowledgment, in its broadest sense, is not. *Generally speaking, a thank-you recognizes doing and an acknowledgment recognizes being.* I hadn't done anything for the woman in the elevator; she acknowledged my being. This distinction will become clearer as you read on.

While most of this book focuses on the positive effects of acknowledging what is good and positive in people, it also covers what is to be gained by acknowledging what is not working with people and situations, especially in business.

Benefits Of Acknowledgments

Like good nutrition and exercise, the benefits of acknowledging come from practice; the benefits of good nutrition and exercise come from engaging in them regularly and consistently, so, too, with acknowledgments.

> "*Constant kindness can accomplish much. As the sun makes ice melt, kindness causes misunderstanding, mistrust, and hostility to evaporate.*"
>
> —*Albert Schweitzer*

Here are some of the benefits you can expect from a regular practice of acknowledging:

Improve relationships

To say that acknowledgments improve relationships is like saying sunlight is helpful to plant growth. The phrase "improves relationships" only begins to describe the impact of authentic acknowledgments. They add texture and richness to the fabric of your relationships. Indeed, something magical happens between two people when an acknowledgement is shared.

I recall being at a new job where I felt insecure about my position. The CEO brought in a consultant who appeared to me as being very pushy and unwilling to listen. We clashed frequently.

A few months into this steadily deteriorating relationship I took a communication course, during which I realized a couple of things: (1) While this guy may have been doing things that didn't work for me, the resistance I was generating had nothing to do with him, but everything to do with my insecurity; (2) I was the only one who could take responsibility for improving the relationship. In other words, if I chose to wait for him to "admit" that he was "wrong," the relationship would only get worse.

I called him, and the conversation went something like this:

> *"Tom, this is Peter. I'm calling to share something that just occurred to me during a course I'm taking on communication. Do you have a few minutes?"*
>
> *"Sure," he answered.*
>
> *I continued, "Thanks. I had been thinking about the friction between us and I realized how much I had been blaming you for it. I realized this weekend that it has nothing to do with you and that I have been opposing you out of my own insecurity for my job. As you know, I recently took this position and I've been concerned about doing well. Because you've often expressed opinions I don't agree with or sometimes wish I had proposed, I have been rather hard on you in meetings.*
>
> *I see now where that's coming from and I would like to take responsibility for contributing in that way to our working relationship. I'd like to acknowledge that our relationship has been difficult and take responsibility for my role in it not working. I'd also like to acknowledge you for your enthusiasm and your courage in standing up to me and for what you believe in those meetings. Going forward, you can count on me to listen more and be much more cooperative. I'll take any disagreement with you offline."*
>
> *There was silence on the other end of the phone.*
>
> *I said, "Tom? You there?"*
>
> *Tom responded, "Peter in all of my decades in corporate life, I have never had anyone say anything like that to me. I have never had anyone take responsibility so completely for something not*

working, with no trace of blaming me, or anything like that. I am completely blown away."

For the rest of our project over the coming months our relationship became pleasant, in fact, almost enjoyable. And in the years that followed, we became friends.

What occurs after an authentic acknowledgment is a connection. A bridge between two people becomes available, and both parties become ever-present to this connection whenever they meet. People become more inclined to share things that they would not have shared before, and to accept contributions as contributions instead of perceived attacks.

It's important to note that in the story above **I did not blame or make Tom wrong for anything**. That was crucial to having the impact that it did.

Improve outlook on life.

Acknowledgments transform the mood, uplifting both Acknowledger and Acknowledgee. There is a great clip called "Validation"[2] on YouTube that demonstrates this very well. In it, you see people in moods of resignation and depression transform into happiness and joy, simply from being acknowledged, or "validated."

"The unique personality which is the real life in me, I can not gain unless I search for the real life, the spiritual quality, in others. I am myself spiritually dead unless I reach out to the fine quality dormant in others. For it is only with the

> *god enthroned in the innermost shrine of the other, that the*
> *god hidden in me, will consent to appear."*
> —Felix Adler from An Ethical Philosophy of Life

The validation video depicts a sort of extreme acknowledgment used to heal people who have rarely experienced being acknowledged. It shows the healing power of acknowledgments, as well as what can happen when they are absent. Acknowledging creates and maintains a positive feeling of goodwill towards other human beings and by extension causes people to feel good about themselves, their lives and their future.

One friend of mine shares the following great acknowledgment story:

> *There is an instance that occurred many years ago that still resonates today.*
>
> *It was in the early nineties. I was running a small delivery company that I had started a few years earlier. On this day, my driver did not come to work and I had to hop in the van and run the business by cell phone. I don't remember all the details, but I do remember that I was not having a good day. This particular driver was not that reliable, so I had done his route several times before.*
>
> *A few of the times I did this one call on this route, a man would be standing on the porch waiting. For what, I do not know. Each time I went, we would exchange pleasantries and smiles. This particular day I was doing my usual hustle to get this job done so I could do my own job. I went running up the stairs to the porch and once the delivery was complete, when I turned to leave he said, "You know, you have great Karma, it can be seen all round you." He then looked into my eyes, smiled, and I said, "Thanks."*

It was a little comment from a complete stranger that has stayed with me for years.

—Chris Elliott

One little comment from a stranger completely transformed my friend's mood and made all the difference in his day and in his life. The acknowledgment I received from a relative stranger in the elevator completely transformed my mood from one of indifference to joy and exhilaration, simply with a few kind words.

Build self-esteem

Self-esteem is the belief or confidence in one's own worth, in one's abilities to provide value for others, indeed that one's very self, one's very existence, provides value to others. Having someone, even a stranger, acknowledge you for your ready smile, infectious laugh, or willingness to help, builds your confidence as a valued member of a social group, family, workplace, or community. Acknowledging what is good, what works about a person, has a tremendous effect on their self-esteem.

In a team management and leadership course where I first learned to distinguish acknowledgments, I had the good fortune to hold a valued leadership position for the whole group (about fifty people) for three months. At the end of each quarter, there was the practice of acknowledgment of the leader. At that time, everyone had an opportunity to voluntarily acknowledge their leader, and it was my turn to be on the receiving end.

Several people took the opportunity to stand up and acknowledge me in front of the group, and I was touched by their generosity and courage. I always mention courage because I think it takes courage to acknowledge another person, especially in public.

There was one acknowledgment that really stood out for me. It was from a man with whom I had had a strained relationship, at least from my side. I found him demanding and a bit hard to be with. He had a tendency to push my buttons. He always made requests of me for things that I didn't want to do, things that I resisted, and he would hold me to account for things I had promised. I had come to realize that he was pushing my boundaries, not my buttons, and I was resisting change. I was resisting my own growth. Without realizing it, I had come to deeply respect him.

Close to the end of my brief acknowledgment ceremony, he stood up and said seven words that I will never forget, seven words that, from him, I know were very high praise. He said, "I would go to war with you." Not in the sense that he wanted to have me beaten up, rather in the military sense that you take the people to war who you would trust with your life. He didn't say much more than that. He didn't need to; those seven words were enough. It was one of those acknowledgments that fortified my inner self, strengthened my self-confidence, and created a thirst to build networks of people in my life who could all say that about each other. It was one of those acknowledgments that I will carry for the rest of my life. Thank you Rudy.

Children

The foundation of self-esteem is formed in our early childhood and acknowledgments are crucial to this process. In the first few years of life, when we are crafting the stories of ourselves and the possibilities for our future, acknowledgments are the building blocks for those stories. The stories of, "I am good; I am loved; I will do great things in life" or, "I am nobody; I am worthless; I will never amount to anything" mostly grow from children's interpretations of events that occur for them as "something's wrong," or from stories they hear about themselves from others.

> *"To value his own good opinion, a child has to feel that he is a worthwhile person. He has to have confidence in himself as an individual."*
>
> —Sidonie Gruenberg

Little children do not have the defenses of adults and easily let in anything that comes from grown-ups, especially those in trusted authority roles. No one needs to tell you to be careful with what comes out of your mouth around young children and to take special care to tell them all that is good about them, yet we often forget.

Please remember, as there is a lot at stake with these young lives: a steady, balanced diet of acknowledging young children does more than improve relationships or make them feel good; acknowledgments actually create their future selves as confident and passionate young men and women, full of possibility for the difference they can make, **or** as fearful, resentful, powerless young people that embrace a life of victimhood or crime.

> *When I was about eight years old, I started building model planes. I took great pride in building military jets and World War II planes. At the time, there was a friend of the family who used my father's home gym to lift weights. One day, I had just finished building a Phantom F-4 jet fighter and was doing an imaginary fly-through the gym. Joe had just finished doing some bench presses as I was doing my fly-by. "Wow! Can I see that?" he yelled.*

I proudly showed him the model, which he took from me and examined in meticulous detail. "This is beautiful," he said. "Did you build it?" I nodded proudly. Then he said, "That's really great work, man! You're good at building models." I remember beaming at his compliment, and to this day I remember how good it made me feel.

Most of us can remember small acts of acknowledgments occurring when we were quite young. Yet for many, these words of acknowledgments never or rarely came from those we wanted to hear them from the most. A steady diet of acknowledgments—including acknowledgments of what's not working (see below)—can make an enormous difference to a child becoming a valued, contributing member of society.

Build team spirit

Humans are social beings. We need each other in order to live well. Even many solitary activities such as reading, for example, require someone else to have written what we're reading. Whether we're going to the grocery, getting clothes dry-cleaned, or ordering items online, we need other human beings doing the things that make our ordinary, solitary activities possible. Wherever we work with others to produce an intended, agreed-upon outcome, we are part of a team, and the mood of the team either helps or hinders the team in actually fulfilling its purpose.

"Feelings of worth can flourish only in an atmosphere where individual differences are appreciated, mistakes are tolerated, communication is open, and rules are

flexible—the kind of atmosphere that is found in a nurturing family."

—*Virginia Satir*

The mood and spirit of the team affects what the team thinks, talks about and does, in the same way that your individual mood affects what you think, talk about and do. Good moods, strong team spirit, high office morale are important because they are necessary for people to work well together. That translates to dollars on your bottom line because good team spirit reduces friction among team members by opening channels of communication, stimulating creative thought, producing initiative, and reducing the need for management. Healthy team spirit is necessary for groups to be challenged rather than overwhelmed, to look for opportunity rather than accept failure, to create rather than let dissipate.

Changing the team spirit is not much different than changing your individual mood. Instead of changing the conversations and thoughts you focus on in your head, we change the conversations and thoughts people focus on as a group. But how is this done when people have devolved into small cliques that don't talk to each other, and no one does anything because they believe they won't be supported and will in fact be blamed when things go wrong?

Group activities are often cited as great for building team spirit, but group activities may not work or have no lasting effect without an office culture that stimulates open and honest communication. Particularly arduous group activities, or even life threatening ones, as in the military, are very effective at bonding teams together because nothing stimulates honest, open, and straightforward communication with your teammates like having your life depend on them.

If you are the boss or the leader of any team, there is something you can do immediately that will start paying sustainable dividends without the cost and risk of any arduous group activity: you can start acknowledging your people.

> *This friend of mine often complained about how his boss was demanding, very critical and never offered any praise to his team. He had placed the team under a lot of pressure to deliver results but made capricious decisions, changed his mind and was mostly unavailable for discussion or support. Morale was very low.*

> *One month the boss was away on vacation and an extended business trip, and left a very seasoned second-in-command in charge. During this month of the boss's absence, this woman did everything that the boss did not. She first acknowledged the existing work load and praised everyone for their dedication and commitment. She prioritized the current workload and focused everyone's effort on those. The other projects would be pushed back to the next month.*

> *Her door was always open and she dropped by people's offices to see how things were going and offer her support. In that month, the team delivered on key projects. But when the boss returned, instead of praising the excellent results on those key projects, he blamed the second-in-command for the work that was not done. Morale returned to its previous low.*

Even if you're not the leader of your team, you can exert significant influence on your team's morale by simply adopting a practice of acknowledging.

Reduce or eliminate envy and jealousy

In her book *The Power of Acknowledgment*, Judith W. Umlas says that acknowledgments deactivate and defuse envy and jealousy. I couldn't agree more. In fact, an office culture that does not encourage and facilitate honest and open communication, breeds an environment where envy, jealousy, and go-it-aloneness thrive. Such an environment kills morale and brings down an organization.

"Perhaps the most important thing we can undertake toward the reduction of fear is to make it easier for people to accept themselves, to like themselves."

—*Bonaro W. Overstreet*

I once worked in an office where the supervisor was clearly in over her head and inept at communicating with her staff. She did not maintain an open-door policy or protect her department and staff the way good supervisors do, so resentment grew within the ranks. Her management style pitted employees against one another to the point where the department was divided into two groups: those subservient to her and the rest who disliked the way she conducted business. Interactions with her were unpleasant and she never praised staff efforts. It became normal for employees to gossip and gripe behind her back about how unhappy they were. Instead of working together as a supportive unit, the department became a tense emotional battlefield as people's spirits gradually broke. Turnover among employees was high.

—*Max Alvarez*

Heal wounds

Acknowledgments can heal emotional wounds recent and long past.

One day, when I was about seventeen, I was out on a driving lesson with my mother. My driving skills were good, so good in fact that my mother was engaging in a rather involved conversation about a matter that she was confronting at her office. As we were returning home a terrible thing happened.

To my shock, as the front wheels hit the low curb that began the entrance to our driveway, the steering wheel seemed to leap from my hand and the car slammed into the gate, completely destroying the left front fender and headlight, all in a split second. I remember feeling so completely embarrassed that I wept. My mother, of course, was quick to take the blame, saying that she had stopped paying attention because I was driving so well and that she should have been more alert to warn me of the dangers of steering with one hand. This just made me feel worse and I went to my room weeping.

Later that day, I remember my stepfather coming up to my room. He looked at me and he said, "Peter, I know you feel terrible about what happened, but it was an accident. No one blames you. No one was hurt and the car can be repaired. That's why we have insurance." He smiled and before he walked away he said, "Come on down for dinner. Your mother made a lovely pepper shrimp."

He didn't have to do that, but his words were like a healing balm. He acknowledged my pain and made it clear that there was no lasting damage. Everything could be fixed and he didn't blame me.

Here's an example of an acknowledgment healing a wound from a distant past:

> *At a seminar a few years ago, I was in one of several small groups where each group member was talking about formative relationships in their lives. When it was his turn this one man began to cry. "I never felt that my older brother loved me," he shared with the group. "He never did anything with me, never hugged me, never showed me any attention whatsoever."*
>
> *"How did that make you feel?" someone asked.*
>
> *"Unloved. Like I wasn't wanted, that I didn't belong."*
>
> *"Was there a particular incident that you can remember where you first felt this way?" asked another person.*
>
> *"No," he said, "nothing stands out, all I remember is this huge vacuum, this huge space between us, there was just nothing there. No affection, and certainly not any love."*
>
> *"How does it make you feel now?" I asked.*
>
> *"Funny, but it really hurts," he said. "Brothers are supposed to love each other!" he cried. "And big brothers are supposed to take care of their little brothers." He choked on the last few words.*
>
> *Later in the day when he had regained his composure, I spoke to him, and he said, "You know the really funny thing is, that realization came from out of the blue, and I never imagined that I had this feeling bottled up in me. Now that it's come out, and I've acknowledged it and shared it, the pain is gone. All that anguish and hurt I felt earlier is really gone."*

> *I asked him if he would share this with his brother and he said,*
> *"No; nothing to be gained there. I don't think my brother had any*
> *idea of what he was doing or even why he was doing it, and if*
> *I shared this with him it would probably devastate him. Whether*
> *or not my brother loved me back then, I know he loves me now,*
> *and what happened today was for my healing. It's got nothing*
> *to do with him."*

> *"People, even more than things, have to be restored, renewed,*
> *revived, reclaimed, and redeemed; never throw out anyone."*
> —*Audrey Hepburn*

Closure or completion is one way that acknowledgments can heal. By acknowledging what is so—how you feel about something that happened, what was said twenty years ago, the meaning you assigned to a particular look from your father when you were five—you can let go of baggage that you may have been carrying around silently for years.

Bringing closure or completing things through acknowledgments is a skill that is not explicitly taught. Yet it is a necessary skill to maintain and grow relationships. Without it, the only alternative is to bring closure to (end) <u>entire</u> relationships.

> *"An intelligent person is never afraid or ashamed to find*
> *errors in his understanding of things."*
> —*Bryant H. Mcgill*

In personal relationships, acknowledgments often work magic. The following example is an account of a father's phone conversation with his son in which he acknowledges his part in their strained relationship. The names and certain details are changed but the essence of the account is intact. It is a powerful example of the role acknowledgments play in bringing closure and setting the stage for a new promising relationship:

After participating in a relationship improvement seminar, John, an investment banker, realized his part in the relationships that weren't working in his life. Taking responsibility for this, John determined to call his thirty-eight year-old son Robert. John realized he had tried to repress his son's creative talent because he had been afraid that Robert would never be able to earn a good living. In fact, he admitted that he had been ashamed of his son's chosen path. He realized that he was choking his son's passion for life and had badly damaged their relationship. He admitted that for years he didn't attend his son's art exhibitions or share them with his friends because he wanted to be right about his son's "mistake" and did everything he could to see his son's artistic accomplishments as a failure.

"I've been so caught up in you doing things my way, and making you wrong for doing things your way, and even more wrong for your being good and doing well, that I kept you away for almost two decades of our lives," John said, his voice breaking and tears rolling down his eyes. "I've been a terrible father to you, and ..." he had to pause for a few seconds before he continued, ". . . and I am so, so sorry. I don't deserve to be in your life or to share your success as an artist, but I want you to know how proud I am of your work as an artist and how proud I am of you just for being you."

There was silence on the other end as Robert wept. Eventually Robert composed himself enough to say, "Thank you Dad, for having the courage to say what you just did. I know how hard it must have been for you. I've always wanted to do good by you. Your blessing and love were all I ever wanted, and right now it doesn't matter for me that it took twenty years. I'm just so happy and at peace now to finally have it, and you, in my life. I'm proud to have a father who could say what you just did, be as vulnerable as you just were, and I wouldn't dream of not having you in the next twenty years of my life."

Close chapters and allow people to move on

Acknowledgments bring closure; they can be the completion to chapters, episodes, or events in people's lives.

When I worked at Philips Electronics in the Netherlands, one of the things I noticed was the company culture—maybe even the national culture—of acknowledging employees and colleagues. Birthdays were always respected, for example. Secretaries often displayed a public list of everyone's birthday and those events were honored with a gathering of everyone who was even just passing by, eating cake and having coffee. As is often the case when people send cards, there is no formal discussion of this practice or why it is done. It just is a tradition that is handed down and followed without much conscious thought.

So it was with my Dutch colleagues. In most cases, this tradition was honored with sincerity and genuine warmth. Years of service and retirements were *always* acknowledged with dinners and gatherings at restaurants or bars, depending on the rank of the person being honored and the number of years of service. People said nice things about the person being honored/acknowledged. I fondly remember one director who was being honored for 25 years of service who commented to the group, "I find it a bit curious that you honor me for this 'achievement' because when you think of it, the only thing I did was NOT leave."

One thing I know for sure: This practice left those honored employees with good feelings about their time at the company and the people they worked with. It was a practice that closed the loop and enabled people to move on with the next phase of their lives.

Things that work, like a practice of acknowledging employees, often fade into the background. You notice it when the practice breaks down or where there is none. I know people who "gave their lives" to a particular company and were not honored when they left. No one acknowledged the difference they made through their work and the people's lives they touched. In these instances, people don't have closure for their most productive times. Without such closure people feel incomplete and have difficulty moving forward in their lives. They may carry this "incompletion" like luggage wherever they go.

"After all I did for them, this is how they treated me," reported one man. "I was responsible for a hundred million dollars in sales," he complained, "and they never had the decency to thank me for it."

In another instance, a woman I know needed to understand why she was never acknowledged for her contributions to her old company. In those situations nothing will suffice but the actual hearing of those words from the people involved: "I want to thank you for your years of service and the many contributions (a few named) you have made. Your work and presence here has made a lasting difference to our growth. You will be missed."

In cases where an employee was less than stellar, some kind (and true) words grant dignity to the departing employee as they transition. Acknowledging them for their service is a small act of generosity that pays dividends in ways you might not imagine. For helping the departing employee feel good about their time with you, your compassion and grace leaves other employees feeling good about working for you. They, too, will feel that their service is being valued.

Allow people to focus on finding solutions

For alcoholics, the starting point on the road to recovery is to first acknowledge that you are one.[3] It's the same for all breakdowns. You can't take steps to mitigate or avoid the effects of a breakdown, if you don't first admit that there is one.

> *I once gave a poor performance appraisal to an inherited secretary. In that appraisal I brought up many of the issues that I had including her inability to produce accurate meeting minutes, her habit of rolling her eyes at my requests, playing music loudly and dancing in her seat. The meeting did not go well as she would not acknowledge any of my concerns as legitimate since in all her years at the company no one had ever said any thing to her about her attitude or performance. This was shocking to me as she was notorious for her poor performance and particularly for her bad attitude.*

> *In a subsequent meeting, through tears in her eyes she pleaded, "How can you expect me to do tasks that I was never trained for?" I was shocked at this truthful explanation of her inability to take meeting minutes. It was unbelievable to me that none of her prior bosses had given her the feedback nor the training she needed to grow. Indeed it seemed that they had done the exact opposite and left her with the impression that she was meeting expectations. They solved the problem that she was by transferring her to the next junior executive. It was my turn and I was determined not to repeat their mistake. It was not fair to the other managers that would inherit her and it was not fair to her.*

It did not work out in the end. Despite assistance from HR, she felt victimized and persecuted and continued to resist all efforts to help her improve. We decided to let her go.

The whole experience changed me, I now never assume a person knows what is expected unless discussed and tasks / responsibilities are clear. I give regular feedback on the good and the bad and suggest areas for improvement always inviting open dialogue no matter how uncomfortable.

—*Melissa Roberts*

This secretary's reaction was understandable, and it's clear that nothing could have been done before she first saw for herself that her attitude was problematic, and that there were performance standards she was not meeting. The incident also demonstrates the importance of acknowledging such breakdowns soon after they are observed. Too often people find it easier to not have the difficult discussion, accept a sub-optimal situation and let it become someone else's problem.

Turns out that the secretary in the story above was a bit intimidating and her bosses were afraid to have what they anticipated to be a confrontation. Almost always the eventual cost is much greater than if the breakdown was formerly acknowledged. In all cases though, nothing can get "fixed" until people first acknowledge that something is broken.

Feel good

Acknowledging people that make a difference in your life simply feels good—for everyone. Even bystanders feel good when witnessing a genuine act of acknowledgment.

Looking for experiential validation that we're all connected? Want to know absolutely that underneath all of our prejudices and negative beliefs about other human beings there is only love? Then take on a conscious practice of acknowledging someone every day. Regardless of race, nationality, religion, gender, sexual orientation, or political ideology, acknowledge anyone whenever the opportunity arises and notice the difference it makes for them, for you, and for anyone else who may be listening.

> *"Love and kindness are never wasted. They always make a difference. They bless the one who receives them, and they bless you, the giver."*
>
> —*Barbara de Angelis*

A healthy practice of acknowledgment sends out a ripple of goodwill and love that affects more than just the person being acknowledged.

In the introduction, I began with a story that demonstrated how good it felt to be acknowledged. Here's a story that illustrates how good it can feel to acknowledge someone else; in this case, a total stranger.

> *One summer, I was on a New York train headed downtown. I noticed a woman who got on the crowded train and sat down across from me. I was struck by her beauty and grace. As I looked at her, I saw her glance to her left and motion to someone. I immediately thought she must be communicating with her boyfriend. Someone that beautiful could not be solo. I leaned forward to see who she was signing to and saw an old woman standing by the door. This beautiful woman was offering up her seat to an elderly stranger.*
>
> *That touched me. And right there in the space between us, like magic, there were words just waiting to be communicated.*

I took out my business card and wrote on the back: "You are beautiful, elegant, and kind. Have a great day."

And then I prayed she wouldn't get off before me. I sweated through five stops. And thank God she remained sitting until my stop. As the train came to a stop, I made my way over to her (which must have looked strange). She looked a bit startled as I handed her the card. And then, I abruptly turned and walked off the train.

My heart was in my throat all the while. As I began walking towards the exit of the station, I looked back towards the train just in time to see her face register the words written on the card. She looked at me through the window with a look of gratitude and disbelief. She was clearly blown away. And then she was gone.

From the look she gave me, I had clearly made her day, and I thought, "Mission accomplished!" as I now swaggered towards the exit feeling "Tony the Tiger Grrrrreaat!"

For those of you who might be wondering how this story ended— did I "get" the girl? and was that my intention?—the answers to the questions are no, and no. There was nothing there for me, but the appreciation of a beautiful, graceful, kind woman. At the time, I did think that I would like to meet her, yet my acknowledgment was completely out of her kindness and beauty. I merely reflected what she projected, who she was being on that train. At a later date, I did meet her and she did confirm the effect my written words had on her.

If you're shy about actually saying the words out loud, this story is a great example of giving a written acknowledgment. Writing it out also gives you some time to think about what you want to say. So why not try it out?

Help make the world a better place

Breaking News: World Full of Fear, Insecurity and Hatred! In keeping with Mother Theresa's stand *for* peace instead of *against* war, your practice of acknowledgment can be your contribution to making the world a better place without focusing attention and energy on what you don't want. A tradition of acknowledgments builds self-esteem, heals emotional wounds, allows people to move on and see possibility in their lives, spreads generosity, and contributes towards building a society where people feel validated in their self-worth and are more secure and willing to trust.

I'm not making a naive claim about a new cultural tradition of acknowledgments as a cure-all for what ails society. All I'm saying is that it's a step in the right direction, a very powerful step. It can be your way of experiencing tasty appetizers of possibility, experiencing a world of people looking out for one another, appreciating one another and helping one another enjoy life. In fact, it could be much more than experiencing tasty appetizers; it could be an essential part of the foundation of a world that works for everyone.

Here's a nice story that I think illustrates my point:

> *Rande and I were on the 79th Street cross-town bus around 7:30 p.m. on Friday evening. An old man in his late 70's—early 80's got on the bus. He was disheveled, hunched over, with his face in his hands. Rande nudged me and said he was the former NYC Parks Commissioner, Henry J. Stern. As we were getting off the bus, Rande touched his arm and said, "Thank you, Mr. Stern, for helping to take care of our parks."*

> *We got off on Amsterdam Avenue. He said, "I'll get off with you," even though he was going further west. He said he was so happy*

to be recognized. I swear he got taller and younger looking
as he excitedly and proudly told us about his NY City stories
newsletter. He asked if we would like to be on his email list.We
exchanged business cards, and he asked about our careers.

—*Robert Gedaliah*

Acknowledging breakdowns, as you do when you give tough or sensitive feedback also plays a major role in making the world a better place as it allows people to take timely action to take care of what matters to them. Whether it's your children, employees, or employer a practice of acknowledging the bad along with the good provides the friendly nudges required to keep a young life or career on track. As tough as giving and receiving such feedback may be it often also serves to bring both giver and receiver closer together in the long run.

MECHANICS OF A POWERFUL ACKNOWLEDGMENT

Now that we're clear about the benefits of acknowledgment and can now distinguish it from the more common "thank you," the question becomes: how can I learn to give effective acknowledgments?

To answer, let's first look at the key characteristics of acknowledgments, the role of the Acknowledgee, and general themes and forms of acknowledgments. Then I'll offer tips on how to give a good acknowledgment.

Key Characteristics Of A Powerful Acknowledgment

This section applies primarily to acknowledging the good about the people in your life and also includes some approaches to acknowledging breakdowns, where you may be delivering unpleasant news.

A powerful acknowledgment:

➢ is Sincere.
➢ is Brief and Clear.
➢ says, "I see who you are."
➢ is Generous and Courageous.
➢ is Focused around Key Words.
➢ is Great at Any Time.

It is sincere

Sincerity is the cardinal rule of giving an acknowledgment. You can mess up everything else in the delivery of an acknowledgment, but if you are not sincere, you are manipulating rather than acknowledging. Be clear on this one point: you must sincerely feel that what you are saying to this person is true for you. If not, you're in the "bullshit zone" of flattery and manipulation, and people can smell BS a mile away.

Sometimes, you may feel it is necessary to ingratiate yourself with others in order to gain some advantage, or influence some behavior that is not working. Sometimes there are strong and ingrained emotions involved. In those instances, acknowledgments are still the best starting point, and I have referenced excellent books on negotiating, influencing behavior and having difficult conversations in the references section of this book that may be more helpful.

Bottom line: An acknowledgment is done purely as a gift to another person, and a gift must come from a place of sincerity.

It is brief and clear

Nothing can take the wind out of your acknowledgment like being unclear about what you're saying. Unless you're completing something from the past, a good acknowledgment should take no more than 30 seconds and can often be done well in 15 seconds or less.

Here are some examples:

"Hi John, I wanted to tell you that I really admire the way you're always so calm in our meetings. You bring a balance, calmness, and willingness to listen that makes those meetings work."

"Patrice, you have a wonderful way of listening to other people's dramas without adding any or becoming defensive in any way. I think that is a gift, and I wanted to acknowledge you for that."

"Nice tie."

"Richard, you are a sharp dresser."

"Joan, has anyone ever told you that you have the warmest smile? When you smile at me, I feel like I'm in a warm cuddly blanket."

All of these are under fifteen seconds. Being short is not as important as being clear. You may need to set up your acknowledgment with some sort of lead-in, and depending on the story, it may take more time. Don't get hung up on time. It's really about making sure the other person gets what you're saying. Being brief and clear is always a good way to start.

Anytime is the right time

From my own experience, some situations call for an acknowledgment: acts of kindness, courage, brilliance etc. Acknowledgments—of the good in people—are best served hot, impulsively and spontaneously. Waiting for another moment often means you'll keep delaying it, or worse, never give it because you'll convince yourself it is unimportant.

Waiting invariably leads to your suffering about what to say, wondering whether you're doing it right, fear of looking stupid, etc. These conversations with yourself are very common. Giving an acknowledgment is an act of courage because you have to go forward in the face of your fears. Don't worry. Be happy. (You'll do fine.)

It says "I see you"

This is perhaps the one key that separates the general form of an acknowledgment from the specific thank-you that we are all familiar with. An acknowledgment says: "I see you and you are beautiful, wonderful, brilliant, kind"; "You make a difference, in your community, in the world, in my life"; "Because you exist the world is a better place"; "I get you"; "I understand you and your situation."

Contrast this with a thank-you[4] that acknowledges an act (something a person did); this can lead a person to believe that they have to do something to be noticed or thanked, that it is their actions that validate their being.

The more general form of an acknowledgment, on the other hand, simply grants their being. Period. There is nothing for them to do or say. It's their way of being or who they are, that we see and acknowledge, which is more fundamental to self-esteem than a thank-you for something someone said or did.

It is generous and courageous

There are no social rules regarding acknowledgments. There are rules for saying "thank you" but not for acknowledging, hence, the need for this book. According to social standards, you don't have to acknowledge anybody. Nevertheless, because of our basic human need to belong, contribute and feel valued, acknowledgments show up, clumsily delivered and uncomfortably accepted.

A practice of acknowledgments is hugely missing in our society. We notice acknowledgments when they happen and not when they're absent, yet assign negative attributes to people who we (un)consciously feel should have acknowledged us, calling them selfish, cold, uncaring, aloof, distant, etc.

Because we lack a practice, or even consciousness, of acknowledgments in our culture, many people are unable to give them, remaining blind to their role in the care and maintenance of healthy relationships. Acknowledging feels awkward; it's unfamiliar territory and any unfamiliar territory is scary. Furthermore, our Western society does not value vulnerability and expressions of intimacy, especially among men. Therefore, it takes a tremendous amount of courage for people who are not used to expressing themselves intimately to step out and acknowledge someone.

Without any embedded cultural conversations about acknowledgments, there is no social pressure to acknowledge. No one is going to hold it against you for not acknowledging, as happens if you don't say "thank you." You don't have to do it because there is no societal pressure to do so. However, when you do, you are freely giving a gift of yourself to another person. This is why acknowledging is an act of generosity.

It is focused around key words

Acknowledgments should be centered on key words, adjectives that strike you when observing the person. You are acknowledging the very essence or nature of an individual. This is often centered on words such as:

honest, loving, beautiful, kind, generous, wise, patient, caring, helpful, cheerful, humble, hard-working, imaginative, insightful, visionary, diligent, forgiving, attentive, leader, collaborative, inclusive, well-spoken, articulate, courageous, inspirational, wise, compassionate, good, good/ great at ..., etc.

A note on acknowledging breakdowns

Acknowledging breakdowns (see "General Acknowledgment Themes" below) is not the same as acknowledging someone for the difference they make in your life. Acknowledging breakdowns requires special care because people tend not to like hearing negative feedback, especially when it is perceived that it is something that they think you are blaming them for. Specifically we are talking about negative feedback as in a poor performance appraisal, declaring a project delayed or over budget or hearing that a relationship isn't going well. Delivering this kind of acknowledgment in a timely way is essential, but blaming is not—in fact including blame will ensure that no agreement is reached about the breakdown and that people spend much of their immediate focus on attacking and defending.

The key characteristics exhibited when powerfully acknowledging breakdowns are:

- A high level of trust exists between the parties involved.
- Focus is on the problem/solution and not on blaming someone for the breakdown.
- Timely delivery—it's out in the open as early as possible.

Trust is already established

High levels of trust between the individuals concerned are essential when criticism and negative feedback is discussed. Recipients of tough feedback are more likely to not take things personally when they trust that the giver of the feedback has their best interests at heart. If such high levels of trust do not exist, then if possible, an appropriate messenger—one who is trusted by the listener—should be sought out to deliver the feedback.

Interestingly enough, trust is more likely to exist between individuals who already have a history of acknowledging each other. In other words, you are more likely to be trusted by someone who needs to hear some tough feedback if you have been routinely practicing giving authentic acknowledgments of the good things about that person.

Focus on problem/solution not blame

Your objective in acknowledging a breakdown is to stop it from recurring or at least reduce its effects. An effective acknowledgment of a breakdown makes people focus on this objective and is therefore easy to evaluate.

You can determine whether the acknowledgment of a breakdown was effective by assessing whether the communication and coordination among affected parties increases or not. If people feel blamed or judged you will notice that they separate into two or more groups that function to attack and defend, which ultimately creates a new breakdown. What a mess this can grow into over time.

Where trust does not exist, people tend to feel blame even when none is intended. If trust is not pre-existing then seek to demonstrate with your actions as well as with your words that you are not interested in assigning blame but in finding solutions and learning from mistakes.

It is timely

Putting off or avoiding acknowledging breakdowns only serves to increase costs down the road. As hard as it may seem you must acknowledge breakdowns as soon as you become aware of them. Reach out to an uninvolved, willing and wise third party to help you if you get stuck.

Taking Responsibility

It is always best when the person or persons responsible for the breakdown are themselves the ones who first acknowledge the breakdown. If you are that person this is wise on three fronts:

- It allows you to control the story before the story about the breakdown becomes bigger than the actual breakdown itself.
- It prevents you from being in a defensive position as you remove any opportunity for attackers to use the breakdown against you.
- It establishes trust in you and your word.

Role Of The Acknowledgee

Up to this point, we've mostly focused on the role of the "Acknowledger," the person giving the acknowledgment. There are also responsibilities/obligations for the "Acknowledgee," the individual receiving the acknowledgment.

You have just three obligations as an Acknowledgee:

1.   Acceptance

2. Gratitude
3. Generosity—Pay it forward

In cases where what is being acknowledged is a breakdown, or you are receiving a criticism you have only one obligation: **do not take it personally**.

Acceptance

First: fully accept the acknowledgment. In fact, it is not sufficient just to accept it, but to **own** the acknowledgment. Let it in. Really allow that acknowledgment to enter your being. **Don't run away and dismiss it**.

Many people have negative self-beliefs, and they resist when another person acknowledges their magnificence. They find it difficult to really let that acknowledgment in. You can see it whenever people are acknowledged or thanked in public. How quick they are to exit the spotlight! Their response casts aside the praise.

Some cultures or families teach that it is wrong to seek attention or public accolades for doing something good. Then, when it comes, we're uncomfortable. People reflexively say things like, "Don't mention it," "Oh, please," "It was nothing." The Spanish say, "De nada" or "No es nada." The French say, "Il n'y a pas de quoi"; the Germans say, "Keine ursach"; the Dutch say, "Het was niks" or "Het was geen moeite"; and the Italians say, "Non si preoccupi (va bene)." It all amounts to a discounting of the acknowledgment.

On the other hand, it is natural to seek acknowledgement. It is natural to want to be seen and heard and know that you matter. You see this in little children. We are social beings who cannot exist without other human beings, and we are hard-wired to want to be seen as valuable to the other members of our social groups, so that we can remain part of the group. It is part of our nature, as innate as breathing or eating.[5]

So, your obligation when being acknowledged is to let it in, like oxygen or food to your body. It's necessary for your health. You are beautiful, wonderful, brilliant, patient …. It's true. Let it in. Sit with it for a few seconds, minutes, hours. You don't have to say anything in those moments. You may feel some tears coming on, and if you do, that's OK too. Your Acknowledger will get that his or her words had an impact on you and will probably offer you a handkerchief, if they're not already using it.

Gratitude

Your second obligation as an Acknowledgee is to thank the Acknowledger. For this, I have full confidence in your ability. We're trained to say "thank you" whenever anyone does something for us. I encourage you to take it a step further and acknowledge how their acknowledgment made you feel, as well as the courage it must have taken for them to acknowledge you. If you're a person who typically has difficulty receiving an acknowledgment, rest assured that it took a lot of courage for the person who acknowledged you to have done so.

Expressing gratitude makes it easy and pleasurable to acknowledge you and almost guarantees that you'll be acknowledged repeatedly in the future.

What the hell, give them a hug! Especially if hugging is not something you would normally do.

Here's a true story as related by the wife of a good friend who witnessed this acknowledgment:

> *At the height of his 1980s success, rock star Bruce Springsteen was passing through a major airport when a man approached him. "Excuse me, Mr. Springsteen," said the man, "but I just wanted to tell you that I think you're the greatest." Springsteen embraced the man on the spot.*

> —*Max Alvarez*

Generosity—pay it forward

Your third and final obligation is to pass it on, either by acknowledging someone else and/or sharing the story of your being acknowledged.

One of the things that I like about the general form of acknowledgments versus the specific form of a thank-you is that with acknowledgments you don't stay focused on the person who acknowledged you. Because you were acknowledged, you are more likely to go out and acknowledge someone else, beginning a great cycle of paying it forward. Just sharing the story of how you were acknowledged plants a seed in the minds of your listeners. Before you know it, they'll come back and tell you a great acknowledgment story of their own. You become a magnet for acknowledgments. All of a sudden, people around you start getting and giving acknowledgments.

> *"No kind action ever stops with itself. One kind action leads to another. Good example is followed. A single act of kindness throws out roots in all directions, and the roots spring up and make new trees. The greatest work*

that kindness does to others is that it makes them kind themselves."

—*Amelia Earhart*

So share what happened and how it made you feel. You now know what it feels like to be acknowledged, so why not give the gift that you've been given by simply describing to others the acknowledgment you received? You'll find that it feels equally as great to acknowledge others as it does to be acknowledged.

Do not take negative feedback personally

Breakdowns, like overdue over-budget projects, inefficient meetings, underperforming or incompetent employees etc., must either be acknowledged or allowed to fester. In fact, not acknowledging a breakdown can be a tacit approval that it's OK. Failure to acknowledge breakdowns will have very real negative consequences in terms of lost time, energy, morale, trust and money.

Depending on the circumstance, a breakdown may more appropriately be acknowledged by a particular role-holder e.g. manager, team member, external stakeholder; however, anyone can acknowledge a breakdown. If you are on the receiving end of such an acknowledgment, in a project status meeting, or a poor performance appraisal for example, your only obligation is to not take it personally.

Your natural and reflexive reaction may be to deny, defend and re-allocate blame to anyone or anything but yourself. Resist that urge.

Nothing is ever 100% anyone's fault or credit, and it is a sign of your maturity and professionalism to let the acknowledgment in and use it to ask yourself questions like:

- "Is this true?"
- "What role did I have in contributing to this situation?"
- "What can I learn from this breakdown to improve my performance and value in the future?"
- "Am I being blamed, or does this person have my best interest at heart and want to make sure I am aware of this situation so that I learn how to avoid it in the future?

This is of course easier to do if the person giving what I call a corrective-acknowledgment genuinely has your best interest at heart and is as concerned about your development as about fixing the breakdown, or avoiding its consequences.

Bear in mind that your refusal to acknowledge the breakdown, or accept any role in contributing to it, makes it increasingly difficult for the other person to remain focused on solving the problem rather than on "forcing" you to acknowledge the problem and/or accept some responsibility. In other words your willingness to acknowledge the breakdown and your part in causing it creates a space for everyone to focus on solving the problem and not on assigning blame.

> *"Success has a thousand fathers; failure is born an orphan."*
> —*Unknown*

Remember; nothing is ever 100% anyone's fault. While a particular breakdown can be directly attributed to an employee communicating the wrong information, or taking too long to respond, it can be indirectly traced to that employee's boss for not providing adequate training, or not communicating the urgency of a request. Accepting your role or contribution to a breakdown does not mean that it's your fault, or that no one else had contributing roles—regardless of what anyone else says.

Your not taking negative feedback personally demonstrates a very high level of professionalism and maturity that signals that you can be trusted. You may well find that your currency among your teammates and superiors goes up—not down—because of your owning the breakdown or your role in it.

Not taking criticism personally engenders respect and admiration, which will prove lasting once you demonstrate that you actually learn and improve from such experiences. This is more likely to get you considered for future projects and even promotions than your denial of what is in plain view.

GENERAL ACKNOWLEDGMENT THEMES

I've noticed acknowledgments tend to have one or more of the following themes:

1. "I love you"
2. "You're good…"
3. "What you do makes a difference"
4. "You make me feel good"
5. "Thank you"
6. "I'm sorry"
7. Breakdowns: Something is not working
8. Criticism

"I love you"

Perhaps the ultimate and most unsaid acknowledgment is "I love you." This one is for the people who are closest to you. In my observation, "I love you" is what's behind all acknowledgments. However, we're not trained to express love to strangers, nor is it necessary to be thinking "I love you" when acknowledging your waiter for being exceptionally cheerful. So I'll speak here about the conscious "I love you" acknowledgement for your loved ones.

This is one acknowledgment that your spouse, parents, siblings, children, etc. can't get enough of. There's no limit to how many times you can say, "I love you" and there's probably no limit to the number of ways that you can express it.

Be clear that your acknowledgments to the people you love are an expression of your love for them. There are many ways to acknowledge people without saying the words "I love you." For example:

➢ Being aware of what's going on in their lives and showing concern for things they are dealing with. Do you show concern?

➢ Doing little things without being asked, such as washing the dishes, taking out the garbage, calling them up to chat, etc. Do you do small things for someone else?

➢ Taking the time to have conversations with them. Do you truly listen?

➢ Being thoughtful; doing things that would make their lives easier or that they would appreciate. Are you thoughtful?

Are you doing any of the above?

Here's a small test to know if you've been acknowledging someone whom you say you care about:

Do you know what that person's interests are?

Do you know their birthday or anniversary or at least have them programmed into your calendar?

Do you know what problems or issues the person is dealing with right now?

"You're good..."

Whether it's playing the piano, fixing things, planning, organizing, visualizing, listening, etc., the people in your life are good at something. You'll notice that when you think of them, you won't have to dig too deeply to find something they're good at, something that you appreciate about them. All you need is a willingness to find whatever it is and acknowledge them for it.

"What you do makes a difference"

Do you think you should acknowledge people for *just* doing their jobs, for *just* doing what they're supposed to? Many people would say no, of course not. They're doing the absolute minimum required and it's only service or results over and above the norm that should be acknowledged or rewarded.

If you think this way I ask you to reconsider. Why?

First, because many people don't feel that they make a difference, they don't feel that what they do matters, and if you look closely you may find people who feel this way surround you.

These people go through the motions at work in order to get a paycheck. They go through the motions to keep their job, to have job and financial security, and their movements are completely disconnected from the valuable service they provide to others—not unlike a mouse pushing a lever to get food.

I witnessed this the other day while watching a customer service representative at a mobile phone store treat a customer with disdain. The customer clearly was a bother to her, and she seemed to have no perspective on the value of her service to the customer and how her doing her job well would allow someone to stay in contact with their friends, family and coworkers as well as access information and become more productive. The idea that her knowledge and willingness to help could make a difference for her customer and employer seemed quite foreign to her.

Second, very few people really have to do what they do. As Joe Clark—played by Morgan Freeman in the movie *Lean on Me*—said, while locked up in the town jail for refusing to follow the rules, "The only thing I have to do is stay black and die!"

We all have our responsibilities, duties, obligations and jobs. People expect us to be responsible, honor our commitments, fulfill our duties and do our jobs, and we expect others to do the same. Yet our expectations regarding what other people should be doing are so great that we forget that everyone has a choice and can choose to do other than what we expect. Everyone serving or interacting with you is ultimately choosing to do so. No one has to help you; not the fireman, policeman, lawyer, plumber or photographer at the licensing office. Every act of service is an act of choice, even when it is not realized.

Fact is, many people don't realize that they have a choice and so give their service or do their work grudgingly. Then there are those who do get that doing their job, and doing their job well is a choice, and they give their service willingly. They're easy to spot; they remain competent at their jobs despite constant change and always serve with a smile. Make sure you acknowledge these ones especially.

In short, acknowledging people for "just" doing their jobs has two great benefits:

1. They are reminded, or maybe get to see for the first time that their work does matter, that the results of their actions are helping someone else take care of a problem, save time, energy and money, fulfill obligations, feel better, feel safe, become more knowledgeable, etc.

2. They are reminded that they have a choice in what they do and we appreciate that they choose to be of service to us, their employer, customer, colleague, supplier, etc.

Every time you see a President or Prime Minister visiting their troops overseas, it is this acknowledgment theme being practiced. Acknowledging people for doing their jobs lets them know that what they do makes a difference in our lives and we appreciate it.

People essentially want to feel like their work is important and appreciated, and giving people acknowledgments for doing their jobs is your best bet at having a highly motivated staff that will stay with you for the long run, instead of going somewhere else where the pay is slightly better or where they know they will have the appreciation they did not have with you.

Dottie Bruce Gandy reports in her book *Thirty Days to a Happy Employee*, that one employee who left her company said, "I would have stayed for a smile." Go start acknowledging your boss, employers, colleagues and the people who serve you in some way, e.g. the waiter or plumber. Your acknowledgment will brighten their day and may make a huge difference in their lives.

> *It was a very cold winter night in New York City, and I had been waiting for about 15 minutes for my bus to arrive. I was standing at the first and last stop on this particular bus route when I saw the bus arrive across the street at the last stop on the route. I was so cold that I ran over to the bus hoping that the driver would let me on the bus even though I knew he would be sitting there for a few minutes before starting his next round on the route.*
>
> *When I waved to him through the window on the door signaling I wanted to come in, he immediately barked at me that I had*

to wait for him to take the bus around to the other side of the street. Annoyed, I crossed the street again and waited for him. A few minutes later he drove the bus around, opened the door, and let me in.

My intention was to ignore him as I walked past because I was angry with him for making me wait. Before I could get by he began speaking to me, telling me very clearly and calmly why he had made me wait. We then got into a conversation about the demands of his job and the changes he's had to deal with during his twenty years of service as a bus driver.

When he let me off at my stop, he took the time to look directly into my eyes and say, "Thank you. Thank you for taking the time to listen to me and talk with me. I can't tell you how much it means to me. So many people just walk right by and say nasty things to me if the bus is late, or even if they're upset about something else. But you took the time, and that means a lot to me. You're a good man, and I hope to see you again sometime."

He then put out his hand to shake mine, and as I left he said, "God bless you!"

I was so grateful for this acknowledgement, particularly because I was so ready to become just another commuter that passed him by. I felt the difference that my choice to simply be present and listen to and talk with him made for him. And I was moved nearly to tears as I walked away from the bus because this experience reminded me that we're all simply people living together in this world, and it's so easy to feel good and make someone else feel good with a simple act of kindness.

Ever since this experience I notice that I'm much more likely than before to really see the person driving the bus and I always say "thank you" when I get on and get off the bus.

—*Bill Berg*

I like this story very much because it illustrates someone acknowledging another simply by giving their attention—by listening—as well as showing how much it can mean to acknowledge someone for doing their regular day job.

> *"If a man be gracious and courteous to strangers, it shows he is a citizen of the world, and that his heart is no island cut off from other lands, but a continent that joins to them."*
>
> —*Francis Bacon*

"You make me feel good"

Then there are the people who just make you feel good. They bring a smile to your face. If you have kids, you'll recognize this easily. It could also be the smiling face and cheerful nature of your neighbor, plumber, dry cleaning lady, doctor, etc. Some people make you feel good, often because their smile, laugh, or way they listen, communicates acceptance and joy at your being in their life. You feel good because they have been silently acknowledging you with their smile or attention.

These are often very emotional acknowledgments for the Acknowledgee as they will not expect it and are unaware of the positive impact they have been having on your life.

"Thank you"

You are already very familiar with this acknowledgment theme. "Thank you" and other expressions of gratitude are forms of acknowledgment. They are often showing recognition of a new situation: a new job offer obtained, a door held open, request complied with, etc. Unlike most of the other acknowledgment themes, we have rules around how and when to say "thank you" as a form of expressing gratitude, and we notice when these rules are broken.

If this book only achieves an increase in the frequency of you saying "thank you," your world will be a better place. If a person's smiling face, patience, courage, makes such a difference for you that your acknowledgment is more appropriately expressed as gratitude, then so be it.

Acknowledging someone for *who they are* and *how they are being* is distinct from thanking them for something they did. This is the essential difference between most forms of acknowledgments and a thank-you. Learning to express the other themes described here will greatly enhance both your practice of acknowledgments, and the quality of your relationships.

Nonetheless, genuine heartfelt thank-yous are never un-welcome.

> *My husband and I are in our senior years and recently we visited our bank where the seating capacity was only twelve. Eleven seats were occupied. We greeted everyone with "good morning" and I took the 12th seat. There were young men properly seated, however, a middle-aged gentleman offered his seat to my husband. He said thanks, but I said to the gentleman, "You are very kind, thank you." The lady sitting next to me said, "That is my husband and he always offers his seat to ladies and men of any age and he rarely gets a nod, but what you have said has made me happy, indeed!"*
>
> —Pearle Phillips

"I'm sorry"

Like "thank you," our culture is also very clear about how and when to say "I'm sorry" or "pardon me," so you probably don't need much coaching here. Saying "sorry" or "pardon me" is actually an acknowledgment. They are expressions showing that you recognize that someone has been caused inconvenience, pain or suffering.

The transformative magic of acknowledgment is easily accessed with a simple apology.

> *One day I was standing in one of three long lines at the local DMV when a business-attired middle-aged woman cut into the line about three people ahead of me. She seemed pre-occupied with the forms she held in her hand, but this in my mind was no excuse to break the line, and in fact seemed like a ploy so that she could. The line was moving very slowly and I was in a hurry, so needless to say this apparent blatant disregard for the rules of civil society began to really steam me.*
>
> *The people in front of me turned from looking at her in disbelief to looking back at those of us further down the line to seek facial expressions of support in return for their grimaces of injustice. This seemed to go on for much longer than it actually did, when all of a sudden the woman looked up from the forms she was studying and looked back at the line, almost like she could feel our eyes chastising her. She seemed genuinely startled by where she was, and she said, "Oh my God! Are you in line?"*
>
> *"Yes!!" came the response from several of us simultaneously.*
>
> *"I am so sorry," she said as she stepped out of the line, "I was so absorbed in this form that I can't understand, that I didn't even notice the line went further back."*

> *There was such sincere apology in her voice that we all instantly forgave her and one man even volunteered to help her with her form. Feelings of blame, irritation and frustration instantly melted away to be replaced by feelings of kinship, warmth and civility.*

> *"A stiff apology is a second insult.... The injured party does not want to be compensated because he has been wronged; he wants to be healed because he has been hurt."*
> —G.K. Chesterton

In the story above you can see how the simple acknowledgment in "I'm sorry" allowed people to see the humanity in each other and let go of a perceived transgression.

> *"Never ruin an apology with an excuse."*
> —Kimberly Johnson

Breakdowns: Something is not working

In life there will be breakdowns. Things that worked will stop working, things that were intended to work in a certain way will not, and people will not work well together because of different perspectives, beliefs, etc. All produce situations called "breakdowns."

Acknowledging breakdowns is different from the typical acknowledgment in that it's not necessarily pleasant, and *there is an agenda*: to stop the breakdown from continuing and/or mitigate its effects. In these cases, you can think of an acknowledgment as a "no bullshit" expression of the way that something is; an expressed, honest assessment of a situation.

A *timely* practice of acknowledging things that are not working is especially important. The sooner a breakdown is acknowledged, the less the emotional (and other) consequence(s). Timely acknowledgment makes it easier to deal with the "facts" before participants make up stories (rumors) of Godzilla-like proportions.

People in authority will sometimes pretend that something is working when it clearly is not simply because they are the responsible party. They will use their words to cover up, pretend, or ignore what is self-evident. They enforce a silent collusion in pretending that all is well, and their co-workers/employees go along for fear of losing their jobs. **There is no quicker way to lose respect, destroy morale, paralyze a team and lose money, than to attempt to cover-up a situation that is clearly not working.** Perhaps you have experienced this in your work environment?

There are tremendous benefits to be gained from acknowledging breakdowns. Things run much smoother and problems are handled quickly and efficiently.

The key to effectively acknowledging breakdowns is **not to blame**. It is not about making anybody wrong. Simply state that there is a breakdown, describe the breakdown and then determine with the individual or group how to correct the problem.

Making people wrong (blaming them) only makes it more difficult to get things working again and triggers defense mechanisms of the listeners. It introduces unnecessary friction because people are no longer focused on addressing the breakdown, but rather on maintaining their status as a valued group member. Things like blame, shame and guilt are unproductive when the purpose is to address a breakdown and move on.

Have any real life stories of failure to acknowledge breakdowns?

or how they were (in)effectively acknowledged?

Please share them on

http://thepracticeofacknowledgments.com/

It could help someone else acknowledge a major breakdown in their personal or business life.

(If your story is used in a subsequent edition of this book I will send you a free digital version of that book.)

<u>Caution:</u> Take care to let go of all feelings of blame before you have the acknowledgment conversation. You may think you're not blaming the person and you're choosing your words carefully while your body language and tone all scream to the person that they messed up, are incompetent, etc. If you don't trust yourself to leave blame out of the conversation, invite someone else to be present. Select this third person based on your confidence in their willingness to nudge you or step in for the person primarily responsible for the breakdown should you cross into blame territory. Ideally, the person responsible for the breakdown should see this third person as being part of the project team or some other involved party.

If you send an email, make sure to get a second or third opinion to make sure it is *situation* and not *person* (blame) focused.

The criticism

Criticism, as it is most commonly understood and used, is the most powerful thwart to self-esteem known to human kind. Yet used correctly, it is an essential skill for any effective acknowledgments practice.

It is necessary to acknowledge both what is working and what is not working. Humans make mistakes and go off track. "Constructive criticism" is an acknowledgment *theme* best applied to assist people in getting back on track. I distinguish "corrective" acknowledgments (constructive criticism) from criticism or reprimands because of the underlying intent behind them. This sort of feedback, contribution or "corrective" acknowledgment should be given in the same spirit as the other forms of acknowledgment covered in this book. It is a contribution to the growth and development of an individual and given within a context of caring for a valued member of your team or family.

Imagine the following situation: Roger, the young trainee whom you like very much and is bright, eager to learn, and great with customers, has arrived ten minutes late to the last three staff meetings. He has apologized but continues to be late.

There are three ways you could handle the situation: with a reprimand, criticism, or corrective acknowledgement.

A **reprimand** would go something like this: you call him into your office and say, "Roger, you were late again for the company meeting for the third time in a row. If that happens again, I'm going to replace/re-assign/demote you, etc."

> *"There is always a way to be honest without being brutal."*
> —*Arthur Dobrin*

A reprimand gets his attention. Roger knows he did something that won't be tolerated, he's clear he will be punished if he does it again. Perhaps the best thing about it is that timely action was taken. You didn't wait for the six-month review to give him feedback. The downside is that Roger is being negatively guided. This creates a context of fear where Roger may begin to associate his actions at work as potentially painful, diminishing his creativity and spontaneity, the very things you and everyone else like about him.

A criticism might go something like this: you call Roger into your office and tell him that you've been observing his performance and that, overall, he's doing a good job, BUT his tardiness reflects badly on his character and is not making you very happy. This is a step down from the reprimand and may even be the step before a reprimand becomes appropriate, but again, it doesn't take the best care of a potentially valuable employee. Use of the word "but" has the effect of negating everything positive that went before and focuses attention on what is wrong.

A corrective acknowledgment might go like this: you call Roger into your office and say, "Listen Roger, I want to bring something to your attention (acknowledge) that is not working. Arriving late to the last three meetings is creating a negative impression about your commitment and respect for the team. I know this is not your intention and I expect that you may not be aware of how important it is to arrive on time."

With the corrective acknowledgment, you are coming from a completely different context, acknowledging a breakdown in behavior, an action that doesn't work, as opposed to something about the person that is wrong. You are also coming from a context of support for Roger. Such a corrective acknowledgment could also be more effective when sandwiched between positive acknowledgments of what is working well with Roger. Showing sincere concern for Roger by asking Roger directly what's causing his tardiness is also a helpful show of support; there may be some serious situation he's dealing with that he's ashamed to share.

FORMS OF ACKNOWLEDGMENTS

Every interaction with another person is an opportunity to acknowledge them. You'll realize that they are forms of or opportunities for acknowledgment when they either don't happen, or are done carelessly or with mal-intent. Here are some simple ways we can acknowledge each other:

Spoken and written

Most of this book is geared towards spoken acknowledgments since the spoken word is one of the major forms of acknowledgments. Written acknowledgments are extra special because the words live on; they truly become the gifts that keep on giving. Writing something down also gives you the ability to get the words just the way you want them without anyone knowing how many drafts it took. Plus, the receiver can keep that piece of paper or email forever.

This is one reason I love high technology. Today, you can email a recorded message—just audio, or audio and video together—alleviating the anxiety of the face-to-face meeting. You can re-record it until you get it "right" and the person can play it over and over whenever they need a recharge. With recording, the spoken word can now live on.

High technology even allows you to send the traditional "low-tech" greeting card. You can go online and craft your acknowledgment (even in your own handwriting), choosing from thousands of cards, or create an original using your own pictures, and mail it to the person you are acknowledging—all from the comfort of your own home and at a fraction of the cost of a traditional card. You can do this at: www.thepracticeofacknowledgments.com

Gifts

A gift given for no special occasion is a beautiful acknowledgment. There is no guidebook that can be complete here on what kind of gift is appropriate, how best to deliver to whom, etc., but all of the same principles of acknowledgments apply.

Flowers almost always make a great acknowledgment gift, especially when it's not a prelude to a request or a make-up attempt after an argument. Whether it is a bouquet or a single rose, the unexpected receipt of either will make a woman's day. Even scooping up a handful of beautiful wild blossoms by the roadside can be an extra special surprise.

Attention—the silent acknowledgment

I once had a boss (in fact he was my boss's boss's boss—try saying that ten times fast) who was loved by everyone in the company. When I met Pat Dinley, he was the Vice-President of Sales. Pat knew everyone's name and also remembered their spouse's and children's names and would inquire after them whenever paths crossed in the office corridors. If he was walking past your office and your door was open, he would always greet you with a smile and many times would drop in to see how you were doing. He was greatly admired and respected. People loved to work for and around him because of the whole culture of warmth, family, and friendship that he engendered.

> "The greatest gift you can give another is the purity of your attention."
>
> ——*Richard Moss*

I remember standing in one of the two very long corridors that defined our office building on my first day at work, my first corporate job in an unfamiliar city, and hearing Pat shout, "Is that Peter Gales?" He was about 100 yards away when he saw me, and as I turned to face him, he continued, "Is that Peter Gales? Is that the new guy everybody's been telling me about? Is that the new guy?" He continued in this way as he closed the distance between us, all the while jingling the coins in his pocket that I came to recognize as his trademark approach.

It wasn't until I sat to write this book that it occurred to me that what Pat did on my first day, and what he always did, was acknowledge people with his attention. I was the most junior person in the marketing department; he had no reason to know my name and no agenda in making me feel special (well, of course he did, he was in sales), but you could feel Pat's genuine caring for people. For him, you mattered. Pat freely chose to give me his attention that day and it made me feel special.

In the years that I worked around him and with him, I saw that there was complete sincerity in his connection to people. He didn't need to know everyone in the mailroom or the accounting department or the IT department or the customer relations department, but he did. And he made everyone feel that they could walk up to him and ask him anything.

People grew in his presence, like flowers to the sun, like young children in the loving gaze of their parents. Pat Dinley is an example of this quiet and perhaps most magical form of acknowledgment: giving your attention.

When you give someone your attention, you're communicating the main theme of acknowledging: "I see you and you make a difference. You matter, you are worthy."

My mother stands as another clear example of acknowledging others by the simple act of giving her attention. I see it all of the time when she's out in public at a mall or restaurant. She sees someone she knows and engages with them totally. She's so 100% focused on them that she's unaware that everyone else in her party has quietly excused themselves and moved on to find their seats or wandered into a nearby store. It's kind of cute to see her become disoriented as she looks around to where they were just standing, completely oblivious to the fact that she was talking for at least five, and often, ten to fifteen minutes. My mom completely gets lost in this person she's talking to. I expect this complete and guaranteed attention is one reason why so many people have come to love her and love being around her.

Listening

> "Listening is such a simple act. It requires us to be present, and that takes practice, but we don't have to do anything else. We don't have to advise, or coach, or sound wise. We just have to be willing to sit there and listen."
> —*Margaret J. Wheatley*

You can't talk about giving someone your complete attention without acknowledging the role of listening. Listening, really listening, is a form of acknowledgment. Very few people have the capacity to completely listen, shutting off the commentary that runs through their head and truly being in the other person's world. You can cultivate this capacity to genuinely listen and I encourage you to do so. Yet some people, like Pat and my mom, appear to have been born with that ability.

The Hug—the killer app of acknowledgments

Hugs are to acknowledgments what wireless is to the internet. A hug says, "I see you and you mean a lot to me." As part of the human need to belong and to be acknowledged, we all need to be touched. "Sniff. Just hold me." Among your friends and loved ones, use hugs as much as possible.

> *"The best gift you can give is a hug: one size fits all and no one ever minds if you return it."*
>
> *—Unknown*

Hugs come in all configurations and intensities. I differentiate between the hugger—the person initiating the hug, and the huggee—the person being hugged. Here are a few common ones I got a kick out of naming:

The overhand: Where the hugger comes in with at least one arm over the shoulder of a shorter huggee.

The underhand: Where the hugger goes in with both arms under the arms of a taller huggee.

The shoulder touch: Where an uncomfortable hugger only contacts an equally uncomfortable huggee via the edge of one shoulder and his arms. Bodies are usually angled out so that torso and hips are not touching.

The full court press: Where the hugger presses the full length of her body against the body of the huggee. This often turns into a "linger."

The linger: Where both hugger and huggee remain in the warm embrace of the hug for three seconds or more. Longer than seven seconds, you're not hugging anymore, so get a room. ☺

Let me know if you have some of your own because I'm a huge fan of hugs. What I like about them is that even when executed with horrific awkwardness, they still convey a message of "I love you, I miss you. I love having you in my life."

If your acknowledgment practice consisted primarily of hugging, you would be doing very well, indeed. The pure, loving energy conveyed by a hug is portrayed very well in the 2007 "Free hugs"[6] campaign by Euro RSCG. Please take the time to watch.

Compliments

A typical dictionary definition of the word "compliment" states that it is a polite expression of praise or admiration. In our everyday use, it often begins with the word "nice." Nice tie, suit, dress, shoes, car, etc.

> *"Too often we underestimate the power of a touch, a smile, a kind word, a listening ear, an honest compliment, or the smallest act of caring, all of which have the potential to turn a life around."*
>
> —*Leo F. Buscaglia*

The interesting thing about compliments is that they are like catnip for humans, even when they are less than sincere. Regardless of the motive behind the compliment, it communicates to the person being complimented that they matter. Compliments work for just that reason. No training required for complimenting, just do more of it, and with sincerity. Sprinkle them liberally among the people you encounter in your daily travels, and don't be surprised when someone comes up to acknowledge you for the joy you spread with your very presence.

Oh, and don't be afraid to speak in complete sentences. Look them right in the eye, smile and say something like, "You have the most wonderful smile," and then move on. You will have made someone's day.

The introduction

Have you ever been ignored in an introduction? Maybe it was at a social event, or the boss was passing around with a VIP and didn't introduce you. It didn't feel good did it?

That's because an introduction is an acknowledgment, and leaving you out of one communicates that you don't matter. Political players and confusion makers know this instinctively and use the introduction or lack of one to very great effect.

When you introduce your staff, colleagues, boss or family to some-one new, take care to include an acknowledgment of who they are to you or your team. Here are some examples:

Your Controller

"This is John Whittaker, our controller. John has been with us for ten years and knows our business better than anyone, including me. Our consistently hitting our financial targets is in no small measure due to John."

Your Sales Executive

"I'd like you to meet Sally Tandon, our senior sales executive handling Talmart. Sally has only been with us for two years and in that time she has grown our business at Talmart by 300%. Not only that, but she's been willing to share her secrets with the rest of the sales team. Sally exemplifies the team spirit in our company."

Your Mail Room Manager

"This is Joey McGuire. Nothing goes in or out of this building without passing through him or one of his people. Last month when the fire destroyed much of our warehouse, Joey was able to get all of our trade show materials packed and delivered on time. He's our can-do guy."

The smile

Consider the smile as the training wheels of acknowledgments. It's easy to do and communicates one of the most basic themes of acknowledgment: "I see you. In fact, seeing you makes me smile. You are a positive ingredient in my day. You make me happy."

> *"A smile happens in a flash, but its memory can last a lifetime."*
>
> *—Unknown*

The smile is the simplest thing you can do in your practice of acknowledgment. Why not try smiling more often?

> *Whenever my husband and I have the need to walk in the streets of Port-of-Spain from the car to the bank or supermarket,*

whatever, (and we always hold hands) unbeknownst to him, I wear a smile for oncoming pedestrians, and I do a short, quick nod. Usually the countenance of the passerby would change and he/she would return my nod with a smile. My husband commented one day, "I find that people generally are becoming more civil, friendlier, than before. I wonder if it is because they consider us 'senior citizens'?"

"No," I replied, "It is because of my smile!"

Seems like a game I enjoy. I plan to change my voice message on the phone to "It's easy to be nice—SMILE!"

—Pearle Phillips

The condolence

This may seem a bit out of place, but when you consider that an acknowledgment is simply the recognition of the truth you will see that offering your condolence to a grieving person is very much an acknowledgment. For years, when my mother would ask me to call a friend of the family to offer my condolences, I would resist. "What would I say?" was my defense. "I barely knew the person."

For most of my life, I had not lost anyone close or even knew very well, and then my brother's best friend died. I was living in Connecticut at the time and my mother urged me to call. Despite my discomfort, I called and a sister of the deceased answered. She was in good spirits given the occasion and thanked me for calling. She provided some details about what had happened, what was happening, how everyone was coping, etc.

As we chatted, I realized what a loss it would have been if I had not made the call. It was a bonding, a sort of re-enforcement of

social connections. It allowed me to feel part of the social unit
that suffered the loss and made me feel like I belonged.

I never asked her what the calls of condolences meant to her and her family, but I imagine it is typical of any acknowledgment: that others cared enough to comfort those who were grieving, and the feeling that the life of their loved one mattered, that s/he made a difference and will be missed.

"Good gossip"—Third party acknowledgments

Passing along good things that someone tells you about another person is a fantastic way to practice acknowledgments. It is the opposite of gossip in that it builds character, reputation, and self-esteem. You can facilitate goodwill between two people who barely know or talk to each other by reporting the good thoughts one or both of them share with you about the other. Before long, you won't need to be a go-between; they will begin speaking directly and doing favors for each other.

It does just the opposite of gossip, which destroys relationships; spreading third party acknowledgments (good gossip) builds relationships. Judith Umlas in *The Power of Acknowledgment* calls this being a bridge of acknowledgment, and my mother calls it being a peacemaker. It is an easy way to spread goodwill among the people in your communities. Blessed is the peacemaker.

At one time in my career, I worked with two senior executives
of a company, one of whom was my boss and the other was his
peer. My boss was a very ambitious and frank person and it
turns out that his frankness often landed for this other executive
as personal attacks. To make matters worse there was someone

in the junior staff that was actively spreading gossip to this executive that served to reinforce his negative perception of my boss.

Many times in private casual conversations with this executive I would sense his "fishing" for corroborating evidence from me about my boss. I never gave it. In fact I went out of my way to only say glowing things about my boss and about his high opinion of him (the other executive), and that his curt or frank statements were not personal, but rather just his personal style. These executives never became close, but they were able to continue to work well together and I'm convinced that this was in no small measure due to my spreading "good gossip" about my boss.

"No one gossips about other people's secret virtues."
—Bertrand Russell

What you say about other people can divide them or bring them together. Acknowledge your motivation for the words that come out of your mouth about other people. What's really underneath what you're saying? Are your words uniting or dividing, contributing or blaming, creating or destroying? Be honest.

Public vs. private acknowledgments

Most people don't often have an opportunity to acknowledge someone in a public forum—at a company or family gathering, for example. A public acknowledgment can be the most powerful form of acknowledgment there is. Done with authenticity and as an act of generosity, the public forum can magnify the impact of the acknowledgment, and often moves others to come forward and express their own sentiments towards the person being acknowledged. Such acknowledgments are often remembered with great emotion for the rest of that person's life.

Love is the emotion that becomes magnified among the persons present. Oftentimes, even when people don't know the person being acknowledged, they are moved to tears because the love can be felt like a tangible force.

Here's an example of one such public acknowledgment:

> *I once worked as a film curator at a small D.C. museum where my job was to schedule independent/foreign art films and documentaries. I loved my work but was miserable because I felt unappreciated and undervalued. It got so that I finally had to give notice because I grew weary of never being given the proper financial support for my programs.*
>
> *One of my last events before leaving the museum was a powerful documentary about an American doctor working in Russia to help young victims of the Chernobyl nuclear reactor disaster of 1986. There were 100 people in the theater that evening, many of them Russians, environmentalists, and physicians.*
>
> *After the film was shown, there was a Q&A between filmmaker Maryann DeLeo and members of the audience, and I remember one woman angrily asking why this important documentary had not been shown earlier in Washington. At that point, a wonderful man named Chris Hanson, who was standing in the rear of the theater, shouted out for everyone to hear: "The only reason this film is being shown here in Washington is because Max Alvarez brought it! He's the one responsible for it being shown tonight!"*
>
> *There was tremendous applause, and I remember feeling overwhelmed by this generous acknowledgement. Afterwards, a*

number of Russian visitors came up to shake my hand, thanking me tearfully for bringing the documentary to the museum. It was a night that will live with me for the rest of my life. That acknowledgement meant more to me than any salary increase!

—*Max Alvarez*

Drive-by acknowledgments

This is perhaps my favorite type of acknowledgment. You can use it with complete strangers or with people you no longer have much communication with because they moved away, took a different job, etc. It's the out-of-the-blue, feel-good acknowledgment, a complete and total pleasant surprise to the person on the receiving end.

One of my favorite ways to deliver a drive-by is via phone message. I will call an old friend with whom I haven't had contact in a while and leave a message like this: "Hey Sonia, just wanted to say hi and let you know that I really love having you in my life. Having you as a friend, knowing that you are out there for me, makes me feel safe in this crazy world. I will always be your friend. Have a great day, babe."

Another favorite of mine is to walk up to a smiling person and say, "You have a wonderful smile."

If I see a happy couple, especially older couples that are still clearly enjoying each other's company, I might walk up and say, "You guys look so happy together. You're an inspiration to couples everywhere."

HOW TO GIVE AN ACKNOWLEDGMENT

It might make some sense to revisit the section called "Mechanics of a Powerful Acknowledgment." The key points to remember when giving an acknowledgment are:

➤ Be Sincere
➤ Be Brief and Clear
➤ Be Generous and Courageous
➤ Focus on one or two Key Words
➤ Sooner is Better than Later

Make sure you have no agenda. Give the acknowledgment completely as a gift of "I see you, and you make a difference in my life."

Ideally, you will be moved to give an acknowledgment. You are struck by a deep insight about someone, and the words will just be there. Words such as *honest, loving, beautiful, kind, generous, wise, patient, caring, helpful, cheerful, courageous, inspirational, compassionate* and so on, are words that describe the essence, being, or very nature of the person you want to acknowledge. Then express those words that come up for you, the words that describe the very essence of the person who moves you.

> *I once worked with a father and daughter in a group environment. Over the course of the day, it became clear that they were very close. Janet was very strong-willed, intelligent, and ambitious. As she interacted with the group, she shared some of her career goals and made excellent contributions. John, her father, beamed all the while. I also learned that Janet was one of four sisters who were all very close and all pursuing their own, individual dreams.*

In contrast, John was as reserved as his daughter was effusive. It was clear that he loved his family very much and was very proud of his daughters, each of whom he had given complete freedom to pursue whatever made them happy. He had come from a family of lawyers, yet only one of his daughters was even considering law.

At the end of the day, we each had an opportunity to acknowledge someone in the group. When it was my turn, I acknowledged John. I looked John in the eyes and said, "John, I would like to acknowledge you for being an excellent father, a father who loves his children very much, so much that he has given them complete freedom to explore life completely and without judgment. You love your children no matter what. I would like to acknowledge you for letting your children know that your love is unconditional, that you love them just the way they are and the way they are not. I'd like to acknowledge you for bringing four lovely, powerful, generous and brilliant young women into this world, if Janet is any indication, and being such a loving father is the greatest gift you could ever give them. Thanks for the difference you make in the world."

There were tears in his and Janet's eyes. My words were an accurate reflection of who I saw in John as a father. It was moving because my acknowledgment was sincere, and given generously.

Taking on a practice of acknowledgments means you also take on a practice of observing and being with people. When you consciously start to observe and be with the people around you, you will notice many opportunities—moments—that are ripe for giving an acknowledgment. You'll notice something the person did or said, or the way they were being in the face of a difficult situation, and the right words—words such as kind, loving, beautiful, patient, generous—will just be there, waiting to be said. Walk up to the person and deliver your acknowledgment.

For example:

To your Human Resources manager who just helped you let an employee go: "Brian, what you just did in there was nothing short of miraculous. You completely made Bill understand why we had to let him go and got him to see how difficult this was for us also. You showed him that you really cared and that everything would be OK. You know, I really admire that about you. You have the most patient, caring way when you talk to everyone. It really makes people feel special and that they matter."

To the new member of the marketing team who has just made an excellent contribution to a persistent problem: "Aaron, I've listened to you speak in meetings on several occasions and I see you have a natural power and style. I think you've got what it takes to go very far in this company."

To the superintendent of your building as you see him in the lobby: "Hey David! I don't see you much, and I wanted to say thanks so much for taking care of that leak for us the other day. You know, I really appreciate the way you are always so responsive to all our requests, no matter how small. I know we can be the squeaky wheel in the building, but you've always been very patient and genuinely helpful. You are definitely one of the reasons we love living here."

To complete strangers: "You have a wonderful smile." "You are very kind."

You get the drift. Take care that your loved ones are the most frequent beneficiaries of your acknowledgments.

When to give an acknowledgment

When you're acknowledging breakdowns, the answer is: *as soon as possible*. When breakdowns go unacknowledged, they fester and grow into bigger breakdowns. The longer you wait, the greater the consequence, which could be any of the following:

- Friendships ruined
- Marriages destroyed
- Morale down
- Projects failed, delayed, or more costly
- Reputations hurt or ruined
- Trust or loyalty diminished or lost

In short, the longer you take to acknowledge the dead body in the living room that everyone's pretending they are not gingerly navigating around, the more the cleanup will cost. A dictator's intentions (like Hitler), a genocide (as in Rwanda or the Sudan), global warming, a car manufacturer's bleak prospects, or the incompetent manager, all become more costly to deal with the longer they go unacknowledged. You have to acknowledge breakdowns at some point, so why not acknowledge them early while costs are low and you can still do something about them?

This holds especially true when you are responsible for the breakdown. You place yourself in an unnecessarily vulnerable position when you pretend that all is well and hope that no one notices the stench or has the courage to say anything. Taking the high ground, not as a strategy to reduce pain, but as a demonstration of your commitment to your word and the performance of your team, signals your trustworthiness to all concerned and removes the possibility of being embarrassed when the breakdown is eventually acknowledged.

As for good acknowledgments, the answer to "when?" is also *as soon as possible*. The real danger of not giving the acknowledgment when the occasion arises is that you may not deliver it at all. The other person is not expecting an acknowledgment so they will not miss it, but you deprive yourself and the other person(s) of the benefit of your acknowledgement. You're not sharing the goodies, and you will have lost an opportunity to build your relationship.

Think of it this way: If the Friday morning bagels were never introduced, there's no damage. Everyone gets their own breakfast as usual and office life goes on, as normal. When you do bring in the bagels that first morning, you bring an unexpected gift. Spirits lift, channels open, everyone feels good. Giving versus not giving an acknowledgment is like that. People don't expect it and will proceed with their lives as normal, but the minute you give the acknowledgment, the world changes. It becomes a better place. The longer you wait to give an acknowledgment is the longer you deprive everyone of a gift.

Too late

Sometimes opportunities present themselves, and if you don't act on them they're gone forever, especially with people you may never see again. For example: someone on that trip to Paris who helped a lost person find her way or a fellow tourist who remained calm and gracious in the face of being treated rudely. If you didn't act and acknowledge them at that time, the chance is lost forever. You will have missed the opportunity to make them feel great, and spread good energy and love. "Not a big deal," you might say, and you'd be right. But as my mom always says, "It's the little things you do that make a big difference."

"You cannot do a kindness too soon, for you never know how soon it will be too late."

—Ralph Waldo Emerson

Use every opportunity you find to offer an acknowledgement. It feeds a continuous flow of good, loving energy in your communities.

On the other hand, consider those times when not acknowledging has a **big** negative impact. Consider the parent who doesn't acknowledge their daughter's ballet performance when it really matters to her, or a son's baseball game when he really needs re-enforcement. Those lost opportunities are gone forever and can have lasting impact on a child's self-esteem, echoed in the choices they make in life. Also, consider not acknowledging your mother or father, then they pass away and you've lost that opportunity forever. How would you feel?

Here's a story about how an acknowledgment that never came impacted a professional relationship:

The producers of a show I had done three years ago asked me to audition again for that same show. I thought this a bit odd given that they knew what I was capable of—after all, I had done the show. I decided to comply as we had continued to be in touch over the three years and they had always expressed interest in working with me again. Maybe they just needed to make sure I was still top of my game and hadn't drastically changed my appearance.

In order to attend the audition I had to change my travel plans and also get myself to and from Las Vegas with material prepared. I was happy to do all of this, and when I arrived at the audition, the producers greeted me with much enthusiasm and gratitude, acknowledging that I'd gone out of my way to be there.

In show business, there is no such thing as a "sure thing," a fact of which I am well aware. So, when I finally found out (six weeks after the audition) that the company had not selected me for this season's show—despite their apparent interest in me and gratitude for my efforts—I was not upset about not booking the gig. Rather, I was quite upset about the fact that they had not taken the time to contact me directly to let me know.

While I appreciated their acknowledgement of my efforts and attitude around making it to another audition for them, their complete lack of acknowledgement after the fact—that is, what appears as a complete lack of consideration in simply communicating with me—left me feeling utterly disrespected by them and absolutely not interested in ever doing business with them again.

—Bill Berg

How often should I acknowledge people?

This is more art than science, so don't look for someone to tell you the precise formula for the number and type of acknowledgments to give each day. If you are surrounded by lots of people, it will be easier to make daily acknowledgements than if you work from home. Experiment and see what works for you.

Above all, do not let this become "work." You can create a nice game of it by sharing this book with the people around you and observing how they begin to acknowledge each other. As others become conscious of acknowledgments as a practice, as familiar as offering a "thank you," a new culture of acknowledgments will begin to appear within your social groups.

If you already journal, you can even keep an acknowledgment log. As part of your journaling, include writing about who and what you acknowledged each day. It can be part of your practice of gratitude.

Diminishing returns

Judith Umlas, in her book *The Power of Acknowledgment*, questions a widely held belief among some managers that acknowledgments lose their power if given too liberally and are therefore best given sparingly for the most powerful effect. I agree with Judith that this is just not true. You only need look at how young children respond and grow each time they hear "I love you" to know that no natural law of diminishing returns applies to acknowledgments.

Judith is referring to the use of acknowledgments as carrots and sticks to influence behavior. While managers are free to use whatever tools are at their disposal to achieve their objectives or promote an agenda, acknowledgments used in this way are not what we've been discussing here.

Don't worry about wearing out your acknowledgments. Withholding acknowledgments harms relationships, stifles growth and could even damage a loved one or a career. If you are truly giving acknowledgments as a sincere and generous gift, you won't overdo it and they won't lose effect. In a business or family environment, acknowledgments are like sunlight to a plant.

Just remember that acknowledgments are authentic and generous. If you are about to give an acknowledgment out of habit, then don't. Hold off until it comes from a place of generosity and sincerity.

Pitfalls in acknowledging

Sometimes you think of giving an acknowledgment but do not, and sometimes you give one that falls flat. Here are some common pitfalls:

The voice in your head

Now that you know what an acknowledgment is and how to give one, you will see an opportunity to give one, maybe your first, and the voice in your head (we all have one) will offer up such useless comments as:

"Now is not a good time."

"S/he's busy."

"There are too many people around."

"I don't know what to say."

"S/he'll think I'm an idiot."

"I'll sound like a sissy."

In the example I gave earlier about acknowledging a kind and beautiful woman on a subway train, the voice in my head almost talked me out of it. As I looked for something to write on, I could find nothing but my business cards. The voice in my head said, "She won't get the acknowledgment because she'll think you're trying to pick her up."

For a second I almost let this concern stop me. Then it occurred to me that she might want to say, "thank you." Whether or not she was cynical would depend on my intent. Did I really want to express something positive, with no agenda? Or did I have an agenda? I was clear that I really wanted to be generous. If she called to say "thank you" and I met a great person as a consequence, that would be a bonus. So I went through with it.

You get the drift. Deep down, you may simply be scared. That's OK. Many of us were brought up in families where you don't say intimate things or offer compliments. We live in a culture that teaches "Don't mention it" or "It's nothing." Many people grew up in families where kind words were not the norm. To diffuse the discomfort, people, especially men, will follow an acknowledgment with a good-natured insult to ease the discomfort of all concerned. Take this example of an older brother acknowledging his younger brother.

> *"Danny you've been a great brother to me, and I'm proud of who you've become." Awkward two seconds follow and then the older brother adds, "And I can still kick your butt."*

Don't do this. While the intent and message will still land to the younger brother, a precious moment is diminished because one or both brothers felt uncomfortable and chose to alleviate the awkwardness with a flippant macho remark.

So, while the voice in your head may tell you to not say kind words to someone, or tell you to add something stupid to mask your discomfort when you do say those kind words, don't listen to it. Go ahead and say those kind words and then be silent. Let your words sink in and be in that moment.

You have an agenda

Remember the cardinal rule of acknowledgment: *do it from a place of generosity*. Having an agenda turns it into a quid pro quo. Many times you may not realize that you're doing this, and your only clue is the awkwardness of the acknowledgment and the empty feeling that follows.

As I've mentioned before, knowledge that acknowledging your boss may help your career may be there when you consider making such an acknowledgment. In fact, you may even suppress the urge to acknowledge her simply because you're afraid that it might be interpreted as an attempt to gain favor.

Don't let such concerns suppress your generosity. There's nothing wrong with being aware of an additional side benefit or bonus in acknowledging someone as long as that bonus or side benefit is *not the reason* you're acknowledging that person (remember the girl on the train). If you acknowledge someone with a hidden agenda, it often falls flat. Unless you are a great actor, people, especially the Acknowledgee, can see your hidden agenda. Your insincerity leaves you feeling empty, and the Acknowledgee puts you on their radar screen as someone who is insincere and manipulative.

> *"Being conscious of the possible good consequences of your actions is not the same as having an agenda."*
>
> ——*Peter Anthony Gales*

You cannot deny that you have an agenda in each role you play in life, nor should you suppress your awareness that a practice of acknowledgments will help you fulfill goals in your career, etc.

There is a difference between having a hidden agenda and being aware of the natural consequences of doing good in the world.

You're blaming the person or situation

Remember, an essential aspect of acknowledgment is acceptance of what is and what is not. The most common hidden agendas are making someone or something wrong, and the flip side, being right. Nothing shuts a person down like feeling blamed. If your acknowledgment did not go well, look inside yourself to see if you were blaming the person. Your words may have been fine, but think about your tone and body language. Blame may have been clearly communicated without you even realizing.

"But how do I give up blaming the person?" you ask. "It really is this person's fault!" ☺

If you find yourself stuck in blaming someone when acknowledging a breakdown or a failed relationship there are three principles you must remember:

1. Responsibility for any situation must be accepted willingly
2. Nothing is ever 100% anybody's fault (or credit)
3. Your willingness to accept your responsibility will create the space for others to accept theirs.

Responsibility must be accepted willingly

"Life is the acceptance of responsibilities or their evasion,
it is a business of meeting obligations or avoiding them.

*To every man the choice is continually being offered, and
by the manner of his choosing you may fairly measure him."*
—*Ames Williams*

You don't have to accept my word on this. If you have kids, manage teams or are simply a good observer of life you will have seen this yourself. Whether it's to make a situation happen or to solve a situation gone wrong, if the person or persons don't willingly accept responsibility they will devote their energy to avoiding, deflecting blame, sabotaging, denying, etc., and not on creating solutions. This seems to be the way human beings work, and it explains why any acknowledgment that really is a veiled attribution of blame will never go over well.

Nothing is ever 100% anyone's fault

Accepting this requires an ability to expand your perspective on any situation. For example, in criminal justice it may be relatively easy to prove who robbed the convenience store because it was captured on video and the fingerprints of the accused teenager were on the cash register. However, if you expand your perspective to beyond just the 15 minutes of the robbery you may consider the gang members that forced the teen to commit the crime as part of an initiation process, you might consider a delinquent father, an addicted mother, etc.

*"The life I touch for good or ill will touch another life, and
that in turn another, until who knows where the trembling
stops or in what far place my touch will be felt."*
—*Frederick Buechner*

You could do the same with something gone wrong at work. A manager or employee may be the one who made the wrong purchasing decision, crashed the system, angered a customer, etc., but if you expanded your perspective you might also consider contributing factors, like this person perhaps being hired despite being unqualified, having been improperly trained or improperly briefed, an impossible assignment, a customer's contribution to the situation, or the employee may have a dying daughter and be working two jobs because insurance coverage was denied...

This works as well for successes, by the way. As the Academy Award speeches attest, no victory is ever exclusively due to one person. Attributing a sole and final cause for anything in our earthly plane is a fool's game.

So if you find yourself blaming someone, try stepping back and considering the bigger picture. What other actions and circumstances contributed to the breakdown? More importantly, what did you contribute to the breakdown?

> *"When one tugs at a single thing in nature, he finds it attached to the rest of the world."*
>
> —*John Muir*

Your Willingness to Accept Your Responsibility Creates a Space for Others to Accept Theirs

So let's assume you can see your part in causing a breakdown that you have been blaming someone else for.

Acknowledging your contribution, acknowledging your responsibility for that breakdown without blaming the other person for their part—even if they had a greater role in causing the breakdown—is where you will earn your stripes as a Jedi master.

> *"It's so sad how we can go through life hating people, thinking that they are so different from us. It is only when we see them at their weakest point, seeing their vulnerability, that we start to realize how similar we all actually are to one another."*
>
> —*Unknown*

This really is about showing your humanity, about being vulnerable, about putting yourself at risk. Being vulnerable is very difficult for most people because we grew up in conversations about being strong and independent. Little boys are often taught to "never let them see you cry" and we associate leadership with impenetrability.

Wrong!

Being human means needing other human beings, and being human means making mistakes and failing. Pretending this doesn't apply to you is very costly; it drains your energy in maintaining a façade, and it separates you from people. Pretending you are invulnerable will most certainly prevent you from giving acknowledgments that heal, or cause people to coalesce around solving a problem instead of avoiding blame.

If you think back in your life, you'll find that the conversations that really moved you—to tears, in fact—are the conversations where people gave up the façade of impenetrability and revealed their human frailty, their weakness and their fears. If you can't remember any, then pay close attention to the movies from now on. Screenwriters milk emotion from this phenomenon all the time.

> *"We all need somebody to talk to. It would be good if we talked to each other—not just pitter-patter, but real talk. We shouldn't be so afraid because most people really like this contact; that you show you are vulnerable makes them free to be vulnerable too. It's so much easier to be together when we drop our masks."*
>
> —*Liv Ullmann*

If you are having trouble with acknowledging others, or with acknowledging your contribution to a personal or business breakdown, this is a place to look. Ask yourself these two questions:

- Have I been unwilling to admit where I have caused or contributed to a breakdown or a failed relationship?
- Have I been unwilling to even consider that I played a role in a breakdown or a weak relationship?

If you answer yes, then the follow-up questions are:

- Am I willing to look for where I played a role in a breakdown or a weak relationship?
- Am I willing to admit where I have caused or contributed to a breakdown or a failed relationship?

> *"When we were children, we used to think that when we were grown-up we would no longer be vulnerable. But to*

*grow up is to accept vulnerability... To be alive is to be
vulnerable."*

——*Madeleine L'Engle*

If you answer yes to these last two then you are being vulnerable,
you are putting yourself at risk; you are on your way to powerful acknowledgment that can instantly transform a relationship and
change your life.

By the way, this is not a recommendation to wear your weaknesses
and fears on your sleeve, but simply an invitation to practice letting
your humanity show a bit more. So go ahead and be vulnerable in
your acknowledgment.

*"People will not throw themselves in front of a bus for a
perfect but cold and selfish demi-god, but they will for a
warm, caring, imperfect human being."*

——*Peter Anthony Gales*

Casual or off-handed acknowledgments

Whether in-person, or a message on voicemail, paper or email,
an acknowledgment requires you to be fully present with the
person, even if the person is not in front of you. If you think they
are expected of you, your acknowledgments become clichés. They
become insincere.

If you are acknowledging out of habit or because you don't want to
offend, you're breaking one of the cardinal rules of acknowledging,
which is that they should be authentic and heartfelt. You can't fake

that. You also don't have to acknowledge the same person for the same thing over and over again.

Break a habitual, go-through-the-motions acknowledgment and replace it with less frequent, but heartfelt acknowledgments at times when you are totally inspired by an individual or situation. You are free to invent what works for you to connect yourself with the person you want to acknowledge.

YOUR PRACTICE OF ACKNOWLEDGING

The danger here is that you put this book down and nothing happens. Sound familiar? How many times have you gotten a good understanding of something from a book or a seminar and then it never makes it into your life? Or if it does, it just fades? That's because what you learned was never made into a practice.

Think of any sport that is constituted by practice, or any profession that is called a practice. There is constant engagement and attention with an intention. In golf, the intention is to get the ball into 18 holes with the least number of strokes. In medicine, the intention is to take care of breakdowns in the human body.

In sports, law, medicine, and other activities, there are many things that shape the exercises, routines, rules, and even eligibility for who can practice. Practice never stops. Whether it's because the body will always have another breakdown or because it's fun to play the game, you always engage with the practice. You never finish. Whether you win or lose the football game, you are eager to play the next.

The more people involved in the practice (not just you) and the higher the stakes of the practice, as in law or medicine, the more rigorous and standardized the practice. The good news is that all practice is a cycle of only three fundamental steps:

1. Story
2. Structure
3. Deliberate Practice

Here's how this might look for you:

Write a Story

Not to worry, I'm not asking you to write a best-seller. All that's required of your story is that it provides the purpose and the passion for your practice of acknowledgments. Take a piece of paper and write out your purpose or intention for a practice of acknowledging. A few short sentences may be all you need for your story. It might look something like this:

- To improve my relationship with my wife/husband and kids.
- To improve my relationship with my boss and/or colleagues at work.
- To create a workplace where everyone loves to come to work.
- To be the change I wish to see in the world.

You can be more elaborate and write more detail to plumb the emotional depths of what's missing from all of the relationships in your life. For example, for each bullet point above you can write out what there is to acknowledge (good and bad), how you will acknowledge, and what life will be like after. You can write out the types of acknowledgment you will give to the people around you, and what you will do to make acknowledging others part of your day, e.g. hug more, smile more, give more attention to people, engage with strangers more…

The story gives you the reason for a practice of acknowledgments. This story should relate to relationships that you value, e.g. your family, friends, bosses, co-workers, people in your community, etc. If your story doesn't connect your practice of acknowledgments to these relationships, your practice will not live.

Structure

After you have created your story, you must next create a structure for you to actually live out that story. Just as your car must have a structure (roads) to drive, and you must have a structure (gym, equipment) to exercise, you must create a structure to practice acknowledgments. Otherwise nothing changes; you'll put this book down, maybe give an acknowledgment or two, but you won't essentially change your behavior.

You can think of a structure as anything that causes you to actually carry out your practice. A powerful structure actually compels you to act for the sake of what the structure was designed to do. Think of the effect a country road vs. a major highway has on the speed of your driving.

For a practice of acknowledgments your structure will be a community of people, as well as some visible reminders.

Community

Create a small community with your family or co-workers. Having other people participating, or at least reminding you of your commitment to practice acknowledgments, is essential to your functioning practice. You can best do this by sharing either this or another book on acknowledgments; acknowledging them first is a great lead-in. Here's how you could do this:

1) Identify the people whom you wish to participate in creating a community where people practice acknowledgments.
2) Acknowledge each one and provide them with a copy of this book.

3) Invite them to play a game of acknowledgments with you (see below).

4) Have someone take on the role of coach or champion for you or the group; this person's main role is to make sure everyone continues to play the game of acknowledgments.

Visible Reminders

You know how you have a meeting reminder come up on your computer at the appointed time to remind you that there's something you committed to? Well, the same principle applies. A commitment to a practice is like any other commitment, and the same techniques you use to remind you of other commitments can work here as well.

Just like you have that reminder to buy the anniversary gift, pick up your daughter, or get some bread on the way home, schedule reminders to play your game of acknowledgments. You can even schedule days when you'll acknowledge certain people. Try even scheduling "acknowledge someone today."

Lists

Lists are great visible reminders to have your practice thrive. Here are suggestions of some lists you can create:

Think of the people you want a better relationship with: your mother, son, daughter, co-worker, etc. Write the names down as a list in one column, and in the right column next to each name write what there is to be acknowledged for each person. Here's an example of what your list might look like. I also included a column to write comments for each person.

Name	What to Acknowledge	Comments
Mother	How much she sacrificed.	She always put us first and I don't think any of us has ever acknowledged how difficult it must have been to raise 3 kids by herself.
Boss	How difficult his job is.	His boss is very demanding, plus he's got a sick kid.
Joe in IT	How much of a can-do person he is.	Every time anyone asks, he's always cheerful and always finds a way.
The bus driver	Doing her job with such cheer and being super-helpful.	She's always smiling. Just seeing her makes me smile.

You could make several versions of lists like this. You could make lists for:

People that are closest to you

This would be your closest family and friends. Think of how you would feel if you knew you would not be on the planet tomorrow and certain people would never get to hear how much they mean to you. Write the feelings down.

People that you work with

This would include your boss, employees, colleagues, support staff, suppliers, customers, etc. Think of what they do every day that works for you or other people that probably no one notices. Perhaps it's good to remind them that because they do their job well, they make yours easier, more pleasant, productive, etc. Think of acknowledging who they are **outside of their work**, e.g. parent, social worker, little league coach, tri-athlete, etc.

Breakdowns at home or work

Are there any situations that people don't talk about, e.g. an alcoholic friend or family member, a workaholic father, an abusive spouse? What about projects or situations at work, e.g. a project destined to fail or has huge cost overruns, a boss that is killing morale and productivity, meetings that go on too long or occur too frequently?

What is there to acknowledge about your career and your financial future? Remember that acknowledgment is the first step to a solution. If you and your team, or family are unwilling to acknowledge that a breakdown exists or is imminent, there is nothing you can do to alleviate its effects or avoid it.

Domains of your life

This is another list option: what is there to acknowledge in each of the following areas of your life? Here's an example:

Domain	What there is to acknowledge	Comments
Health	My eating habits are not good and will cause me major health problems in ten years if I don't change them.	I eat lots of sweets, and I smoke.
Spirituality	My spiritual/religious practices are strong, and the source of peace and fulfillment in my life.	I owe this to my father, and I will acknowledge him for it.
Money	I have not been saving and investing enough, in fact I have been avoiding even knowing what my financial targets are. I need help.	If I continue this way I won't be able to send my kids to college, or retire.
Career	I have not taken responsibility for my career and will remain stuck in my current job or get fired if I don't take action now.	I have stopped trying because I felt overlooked and underappreciated when I was passed over for the last promotion.

Create one list or many, but do create a list to start with. Remember that a practice of acknowledgments is as much about what's good as about what's bad in relationships and situations. You probably know immediately all that is bad, but a list can help you think about what's good that you have yet to acknowledge.

Deliberate Practice—Invent and Play a game of Acknowledgment

In most cases, the mere doing of an activity is not enough to improve at it. Take playing tennis, the piano or even just typing. Only focused attention on what it takes to get better (deliberate practice[7]) ensures improvement. However, since no standards exist for world-class acknowledgment performance it's sufficient to just make a game of it and observe your results.

The relationship of practice to games is well understood and perfectly applicable here. Making it fun is also helpful. Here are five games to engage others in the practice of acknowledgments, transforming your workplace and your family in as little as a single day:

- At dinner each evening, have everyone take a turn acknowledging someone in the family.
- In the workplace, have co-workers acknowledge someone on the team at your weekly meetings.
- Include an acknowledgment of your family member, teammate, employee etc. whenever introducing them to someone.
- Make a game of paying acknowledgments forward, meaning that the person receiving an acknowledgment commits to acknowledging someone else within a specific time frame no longer than twenty-four hours.
- Take on acknowledging one person at a time for a ten-, twenty- or thirty-day period.

There are other games you can invent, just keep the practice alive by actually playing your game of acknowledgments, and like any game, keep track of the results you get. Are people lighting up? Are you? If not, what's missing? What could you do differently? What are you learning about yourself that may be holding you back from acknowledging sincerely and generously, the people in your life?

Here are some signs that your practice of acknowledgments is working:

- People at work or home are cheerful, smiling and optimistic.
- People are approachable and unafraid to approach you for your opinions and advice.
- People are more cooperative and work well together.
- People are more willing to drop what they are doing to help you.
- You are genuinely more appreciative and caring about the people around you.
- You are noticing really amazing qualities in the people around you.

Summary

The key actions for your practice of acknowledgments are:

1) Write down what you see for yourself out of a practice of acknowledgments; this can be as simple as a few basic sentences.
2) Create a community of people, family and/or co-workers, people you interact with, by first acknowledging them individually and then sharing this book with them (see books by B. Gandy and J. Umlass referenced at the end of this book).
3) Have someone take on the role of coach or champion for you or the group. This person's main role is to make sure everyone continues to play the game of acknowledgments.
4) Create a list or lists of people and situations to acknowledge.
5) Invent a game of acknowledging with your community and play it at a specific time every day/week as part of some pre-existing gathering or meeting, e.g. family dinner or Monday morning business meetings.
6) At least once a month, discuss the game and the effects it is producing. Make any necessary changes under the guidelines of your coach or champion.

Over time, the effort to engage with the practice becomes less and less. On an individual level we say that it has become a habit, on an organizational or group level we say this is the culture.

Please visit www.thepracticeofacknowledgments.com/ for support with your practice of acknowledgments. There you'll be able to read stories of acknowledgments, share your own as well as send written acknowledgments to the people in your life. You can also reach out to me and the community there with any questions you might have.

Key Questions To Ask Yourself When Preparing To Acknowledge

I wince a little as I write this section. It makes the act of acknowledging seem burdensome, like a huge task to prepare for, when it's not at all like that (unless you are acknowledging a breakdown). For me, the best acknowledgments are spontaneous opportunities that arise when you connect with the soul of a person. You look into their eyes and see beauty, kindness, even hurt, and in that moment there is something to be said, something is there, waiting to be acknowledged. Sometimes they become someone extraordinary in the face of a difficult situation, and the words expressing what they have done or become—to deal with that situation—arise naturally for you to express to that person.

> *"Treat people as if they were what they ought to be and you help them to become what they are capable of being."*
> —*Johann Wolfgang von Goethe*

When you work with teams, or around any group of people who act towards the fulfillment of some objective, you might need to more actively create opportunities for acknowledgments. If the words don't come naturally, ask yourself the following questions about that person/group:

- What does this person do well? What do they do very well?
- What does this team do well? What does the team do very well?
- Is there something that this person is struggling with silently?
- What qualities does s/he bring when s/he walks into a room?
- What can you say about this person's work style?
- Does this person play well with others?

- What can you say about her concern for and actions with her friends, colleagues?
- Who is this person in other areas of life that you don't see, e.g. is she a community leader, a good mother, a tri-athlete?

If your answers to these questions are criticisms and negative feedback you still have something to acknowledge—just not the positive acknowledgment that you may have been hoping for. If you have to work very hard to come up with a reason to acknowledge something positive in someone, then you probably ought to be asking yourself different questions, such as: "Why do I have this person in my life?" and "Would my life be better with this person out of it?" Yes, some acknowledgments can end relationships, romantic or professional, but handled well and in a timely manner they can still leave people with dignity, respect, and closure so that they can move on with their lives.

Find Your Style

The cardinal rule of acknowledging is that it must have no agenda other than your complete generosity. While everyone is capable of extreme generosity, not everyone can access this easily. How you access your generosity and authenticity depends a lot on your style. If you're better with the written word, then by all means, use paper and pen or a keyboard to deliver your gifts of acknowledgments. If you feel more comfortable with humor, then use that to help you break the ice. If you're comfortable with public acknowledgments, do that.

A LIFE PRACTICE OF ACKNOWLEDGING

In my life, the best example of someone who has always had an active practice of acknowledging is my mother. To convey a true sense of my magnificent mother and give you a window into her practice of acknowledgments, I will share a bit of what makes her special.

My mother has always been the go-to person. From her colleagues and bosses to her friends and family and even their friends and family, Pearle is the one person people go to when they want to get things done.

Even now, in retirement, her neighbors often turn to her to solve some issue they've tried unsuccessfully to resolve. Pearle would call the relevant government agency and ask to speak to someone she knows, or simply "chat up" whomever she gets on the other end of the line. In the end, and entirely over the phone, my mother would reach a decision maker who would hear her case and take action.

While my mother's stories can teach a lot about sales, networking and influence, I'll focus on how her practice of acknowledgment was and continues to be the source of her extraordinary ability to get things done.

Averse to any attention on herself, my mother is quick to acknowledge and thank anyone who crosses her path. In her home country where customer service is rare, my mother is quick to praise and acknowledge not just the service provider, but also that person's boss. A believer in random acts of kindness, Pearle trusts that little things in life make a huge difference; more importantly, she is vocal about them when she sees them.

Ironically enough, only when I began to distinguish acknowledgments as a social phenomenon offering many benefits as outlined in this book did I realize that my mother had been practicing acknowledgments all her life, and that this practice had allowed her to be so influential in getting things done.

Please remember that the one cardinal rule of an acknowledgment is that there must be no agenda other than to feel good. It is not flattery. Flattery is when you tell someone something that may or may not be true with the express purpose of them becoming favorably disposed towards you. Insincerity transmits just as loudly as sincerity. People can detect both, just as they can tell the difference between perfume and bullshit (the biological kind). Flattery and insincerity are not Pearle's way.

Pearle's acknowledgments have always been authentic. She lets people know that she noticed that they cared, listened, went over and above, or simply smiled and helped everyone feel good about a situation. There is no escaping her when she notices kindness. She is also able to transform uncaring and thoughtless behavior into thoughtful, helpful and grateful behavior, even if also slightly sheepish.

Here in her own words are seven short descriptions of what makes up her acknowledgment practice:

1. Whenever I visit any business place or Government office and receive excellent service from an employee, I always ask his/her name and the name of the supervisor. I later phone and express my appreciation for the service rendered by the employee (by name). I ask that supervisor to extend my thanks to (name). I do the same for persons who provide information

over the phone. I first say, "thank you" and then ask the name. I then speak to the supervisor, as well. I get a great deal of satisfaction doing this.

2. Whenever someone makes a complimentary statement about a mutual friend, I ask permission to relay that information to the friend. I usually phone the friend and say, "Let me make your day." And proceed to tell her/him what was said and also add my own compliments. The friend always expresses pleasure at the news.

3. Many times in conversation with my husband we talk about a situation, and the thought would crop up on how a friend or relative has a great sense of humor and how happy we always feel to be in his/her company. I would often phone and relay our good thoughts.

4. I make a point of saying thank you to attendants in restaurants, salespersons, cashiers, and anyone who provides even the most menial service. On entering any building, I always greet security officers; on departure I bid farewell and thanks, or say "Have a good evening/day." I am always gratified by their response.

5. On entering an elevator, I always say good-morning/evening. Very seldom do I hear a choir reply. I do not do a roll call, but I often hear at least one voice, so I know there is at least one person who is happy with him/herself.

6. I have noticed that when people are about to pass through a heavy metal swinging door in an office building, most people coming from the opposite direction push the door and try to pass you hurriedly. You then have to scamper to hold the door open. However, when that person briefly holds the door for me, but is clearly in a hurry to let go, I beat them to it with, "Thank you so much," or sometimes say to the men, "Chivalry is not dead." The stunned door-pusher usually hesitates and actually stands holding the door open for me because I said, "Thank

you." They feel great and so do I! I am then confident that he/ she will continue to hold doors for others.

7.   Upon entering a room, such as a doctor's office or anywhere that persons are convened, I usually say, "Good morning/day/ evening" in a clear tone of voice so that all could hear. It's a good feeling to get replies.

> *"People will forget what you said, they will forget what you did, but they will never forget how you made them feel."*
>
> —*Maya Angelou*

A word on PERFORMANCE APPRAISALS

The dreaded performance appraisal. Most people look forward to performance appraisals with as much enthusiasm as a root canal. Except in this case, the dentist hates the procedure just as much. Why is this?

> *"Communication leads to community, that is, to under- standing, intimacy and mutual valuing."*
>
> —*Rollo May*

First, consider that a performance appraisal is essentially a formalized acknowledgment of an employee's performance since the last ap- praisal. Two people, one in the role of boss and the other in the role of employee, sit together to acknowledge how they each see the employee's performance, with the intent of coming to a formalized common view that will affect the employee's career and salary.

Because performance appraisals are not freely given, not done as an act of generosity, and have such powerful real-world consequences for the livelihood of the employee, they are not acknowledgments in the way we have framed acknowledgments in this book.

However, acknowledgments, or rather the lack of acknowledgments, is the major contributing factor to why performance appraisals consistently make so many participants uncomfortable. Consider that a performance appraisal is often the only instance of feedback or acknowledgment shared with the employee. The poor soul is working her very best, yet receives no clear acknowledgment of her performance, neither good nor bad, until the dreaded appraisal.

This is very common because most people are not formally taught or encouraged to acknowledge others as part of their normal day-to-day interactions with their fellow human beings. The boss is reluctant to give an acknowledgment because s/he is generally uncomfortable with acknowledgments and may be particularly uncomfortable with acknowledging a breakdown. So it is put off until the performance appraisal.

Consider that routinely acknowledging colleagues and employees, as well as timely acknowledgment of breakdowns—a practice of acknowledgments—will have the added benefit of making performance appraisals much more agreeable to all concerned because there will be no surprises. The employee will already know where s/he stands with the boss and no one will be shaking in their shoes.

In other words, a practice of acknowledgments can make your performance appraisals go much more smoothly and agreeably for all concerned; reason enough to start your practice now? ☺

Lastly, in your performance appraisals have the courage to acknowledge breakdowns in performance, competence and attitude. While it may seem easier to avoid having the difficult conversation, you only serve to delay the inevitable and incur unnecessary cost and pain until the time they become too much for you and your organization to bear. Your failure to address performance, competence and attitudinal issues may well cost you your highly-valued employees.

"Always leave people with their sense of dignity, and never underestimate their need for it."

——*George Plimpton*

AN ACKNOWLEDGMENT TO YOU

In conclusion, I would like to acknowledge you for being an explorer, someone willing to look and discover. I would like to acknowledge you for being open to new ideas, and I'd like to acknowledge you as someone willing to make a difference. There are lots of things not working in this world, and we need people like you to make a difference with integrity of character and generosity of spirit.

The impact of words cannot be overstated. They should be treated with reverence for they have the power to build or destroy, and it is only with conscious attention that we can use them to heal and create. You can make a difference, and it's easier than you think. As Gandhi said: "Be the change you wish to see in the world."

If you wish the world to be a place where our sons and daughters can be safe to walk the streets and grow up to accomplish magnificent things in a world that seeks the value in different perspectives, cultures, religions, etc., then simply start acknowledging all that is good around you. You'll find that you'll experience a lot more of the good in life when you start acknowledging the people who help make it so.

Please visit www.thepracticeofacknowledgments.com where you can read stories of acknowledgments, get the latest tips and techniques, as well as have personalized acknowledgments delivered to the homes of the people in your life. If you're willing to have your story of acknowledgment featured in the next edition of this book, I'll be happy to send you a free digital copy of the book. Just submit it at www.thepracticeofacknowledgments.com

I wish for you long life in health, happiness, and prosperity. When you finally pass on, may you be remembered for your accomplishments, and for how good you made people feel.

Have true stories of acknowledgments to share?

Want to send acknowledgments to loved ones and business associates?

Want to learn more about how to use acknowledgments to build relationships?

Visit:

http://thepracticeofacknowledgments.com

(If your story is used in a subsequent edition of this book I will send you a free digital version.)

FAQ'S

Q: How do I know what to acknowledge?

A: Notice the people around you and the qualities that they have: beauty, grace, humility, efficiency, dignity, clarity, focus, enthusiasm, humor, restraint, speed, method ... the list goes on. Pick the words that best describe what strikes you about the person. You will not have to search very hard to find what there is to acknowledge. After all, an acknowledgment is the recognition of what already is. Once you recognize it, articulate it to that person. I've found two adjectives are more than enough in most cases, although if several flow naturally, then let them.

Q: How do I know if I'm doing it right?

A: Observe how you feel before and after you give an acknowledgment. A successful acknowledgment is easy to assess because both you and the person being acknowledged will be moved. If not, then likely one thing was missing that should have been there (authenticity), and/or one thing was there that should not have been (agenda). Don't bother too much about getting it right. It's more important that you're in the game, on the field, giving acknowledgments. You'll find what works for you.

Q: Should I wait for the person to be alone? Does it matter if other people are around when I give the acknowledgment?

A: You'll probably feel more comfortable giving the acknowledgment when you have a private moment with the Acknowledgee.

That way you can best take care of your nervousness and spare that person any awkwardness if they are not used to being acknowledged or harbor feelings of unworthiness. This is not a hard and fast rule, though. At company functions, parties and award ceremonies, public acknowledgments are called for and expected. Evaluate the situation and what you want to acknowledge the person for, then decide if it's appropriate to acknowledge them publicly.

Q: What's the difference between an acknowledgment and a compliment?

A: A compliment is a form of acknowledgment. It's very casual and the easiest form to give. "Nice tie," is a compliment. They can be freely and liberally given, just be careful that you are sincere when giving them. Flattery is insincere and is usually obvious to the recipient.

Q: Can my practice of acknowledging also include "thank you"?

A: Certainly. Do not let the theoretical difference between the two stop you. It's OK when you use the words "thank you" in an acknowledgment. You won't lose points and you may find yourself defaulting to those two words simply because in our popular culture they have a more established place than "I'd like to acknowledge you for …"

Q: I feel silly giving an acknowledgment. Why is that?

A: Good that you're paying attention to how you feel. There could be many things behind feeling awkward. Check to see if you have an agenda, or if you're listening to the voice in your head. The latter will often be second guessing you and hence make you feel silly. Just let that go and give the acknowledgment anyway.

Q: I was being generous and authentic, but the person I acknowledged didn't seem to be moved. He seemed uncomfortable and that made me uncomfortable. What went wrong?

A: Perhaps nothing, except that you may have let his discomfort get to you. Don't forget that some people find it very difficult to accept an acknowledgment. So many people harbor feelings of unworthiness that they experience your acknowledgment as a disconnect. Psychologists call it cognitive dissonance. They cannot reconcile your acknowledgment of them with their negative self-image and they react by pushing it away, feeling awkward, and running away. Don't worry about it and by all means continue your practice of acknowledging.

Q: I'm afraid that if I acknowledge something that is not working at my job, I'll be fired.

A: Too bad. That's a sign of an unhealthy work environment and a business that is likely to miss objectives and perform poorly. I have experienced business situations where everyone talked "at the water fountain" about projects that were going to fail yet were never acknowledged in management meetings where they were spoken about as merely "delayed." Look first to your commitment to the company and your own integrity. If you really feel that you can't speak out and acknowledge what you know to be the case, then I would advise you to look for work elsewhere.

Q: Are there some persons for whom this doesn't work? Are there some people who can't give or receive acknowledgments?

A: No, but it sure feels that way. ☺ You can't get people to give acknowledgments and many people start off feeling very uncomfortable receiving acknowledgments. There are cultural reasons and individual reasons that account for both. My guess is that the people with low EQs (emotional intelligence) may have a hard time giving acknowledgments, and they may need to spend some time on the receiving end where they learn to let in or allow the feelings of love, acceptance, self-worth and healing to build. Only then will they be able to authentically give an acknowledgment.

Q: Is a roast an acknowledgment?

A: A roast is the North American tradition of subjecting an individual to a mixture of public insults and praise. The stories told about that individual can be untrue, but the roast is meant to high-light that individual's accomplishments and good nature. For the truly accomplished and abundantly confident person a roast can be an excellent acknowledgment. Even so, there is always the danger of crossing the line and humiliating someone with a story that they would have preferred remained private. I would not recommend doing a roast of the average person for this reason. True profes-sionals do roasts of the stars on TV and to be in show business you must have thick skin. This is not the case for the average person. So yes, I think a roast is an acknowledgment, and a very risky way of delivering said acknowledgment. If you do wish to go this route, I would advise you to clear every speech by someone very close to that person

Q: I can't think of what to acknowledge in this person. In fact, when I think of the person, unkind thoughts keep coming up. I know acknowledgments can make a difference in our relationship, but how can I find something to acknowledge?

A: First, exhale! You don't have to acknowledge everyone in your life. If this person is very important to you, then take a look at what you're holding on to. Very likely, you're holding on to blaming them for something and could take a look at letting go of your blame and resentment. In case you didn't know, forgiveness is something you do for yourself and not any sort of get-out-of-jail-free card bestowed on an undeserving person. Read *the Sedona Method* by Hale Dwoskin for more on this.

Seek and you shall find. If you genuinely seek to find the good in someone you will. If you can't find anything it means you've judged them/written them off.

You could also start by acknowledging *your* role in why your relationship is not good instead of looking for something about them that you admire. You may find that they will be so moved by your being vulnerable that they will open up to you in a way that would not be possible otherwise. (Remember John's conversation with his artist-son, Robert, and my conversation with Tom?)

A word of caution: if the relationship is sufficiently poisoned or negative perceptions of both parties entrenched, the Acknowledgee will need some reason to trust your sincerity, be it your religious conversion, epiphany from a book, discovery of a terminal illness, etc. Without such a reason to trust your generosity, the Acknowledgee may not be able to believe your sudden change of behavior.

ABOUT THE PRACTICE OF YOUR LIFE

Many people live from a context that there's something wrong—especially with them—and if they just did that one (or two or three) thing(s), life would be great. All they have to do is find it or figure it out.

Maybe they think they need to quit their job, get that promotion, start their own business, win the lottery, learn to invest in real estate, get married, etc. Once they accomplish that "thing," life will be great and they can live "happily ever after." They are constantly on the lookout for the magic pill that will cure all of life's ills, moving from hope to disappointment, building a thick skin of skepticism, and even cynicism, as they become resigned to their lot.

For people who live from the idea that life should not have problems, that failure and breakdowns are bad, or that they can (and should) do it on their own, it is a sign of weakness to ask for or be given help.

Living your life as a practice means expanding the concept of practice in sports, music or profession to encompass your entire life. Living your life as a practice allows you to see that you live from within a particular framework, even when you may not be aware of it.

It's obvious that when you want to improve at anything, you practice. What's not so obvious is that it's the *commitment* to the practice itself that makes the great players, musicians, doctors, lawyers, etc. For coach John Wooden, the "winningest" coach in college basketball, it was the practice sessions where games were won and great players created.[8]

It is in practice that you develop the skill to deal with the unforeseen. It is in practice that you develop the capacity to adapt to what the game throws at you.

In sports, music, or business, you will notice that the player—the practitioner—is committed to whatever it is he or she is famous for. They love to play and win at their game. They have a level of commitment to their game that most people do not. Clearly, the love and commitment to the practice is just like any other relationship; there are ups and downs, and sometimes even a desire to quit. Reinventing the practice, or your commitment to it, is also part of the practice.

If you're committed to having a great life, there's a lot you can learn from famous players in sports, music and business.

To use the analogy of sports, the Practice of Your Life is the game of your life. You strive to improve throughout the course of your life by doing the drills, playing for the championships, getting the best coaches and teammates, developing the discipline, skill, passion and burning desire to be the best at your game. In short, utilizing much of what great athletes call *practice* can also help you win at your game of life.

Living your life as a *practice* allows you to create the routines, drills, and exercises that constitute whatever it takes for you to become good at your game. This philosophy is different from most of the self-help and personal growth ideas you may be familiar with because this does not promise a quick fix for your life. There's no substitute for dedicated, disciplined, concentrated practice to have the experience of being able to perform when you need to, and deliver results that matter.

Have you taken the time to consider what the game of your life is? Or have you been on the sidelines for so long that you can't even imagine it's a game you can win anymore?

Please visit www.the practiceofyourlife.com to learn how you can get more out of life by living yours as practice.

NOTES

1 Source: The Greeting Card Association http://www.greeting-card.org/about.php?ID=2. IBISWorld reported the industry's 2009 revenues as $10.7 billion usd. http://www.ibisworld.com/industry/default.aspx?indid=1235

2 "Validation"(http://www.youtube.com/watch?v=Cbk980jV7Ao) is a fable about the magic of free parking. Starring TJ Thyne & Vicki Davis. Writer/Director/Composer - Kurt Kuenne.

3 http://en.wikipedia.org/wiki/Twelve-step_program# References

4 Strictly speaking, a thank-you is an acknowledgment, however it is a specific form of acknowledgment sufficiently different from the general form of an acknowledgment; I contrast the two only to highlight that there is no quid quo pro in most acknowledgments.

5 Go to http://en.wikipedia.org/wiki/Maslow%27s_hierarchy_of_needs for a quick overview of Maslow's hierarchy of need.

6 (http://www.youtube.com/watch?v=9O6vZTvQl4o) "Free hugs" campaign by Euro RSCG.

7 Very simply stated, deliberate practice focuses on inventing and performing exercises to eliminate mistakes and establishing proper technique with the help of a teacher and coach. You can learn more about deliberate practice at www.thepracticeofyourlife.com and the paper on "The Role of Deliberate Practice in the Acquisition of Expert Performance" by Ericsson.

8 John Wooden on True Success at Ted.com. Filmed Feb 2001, posted Mar 2009 http://www.ted.com/talks/lang/eng/john_wooden_on_the_difference_between_winning_and_success.html

BIBLIOGRAPHY

CARNEGIE, Dale. How to Win Friends & Influence People. Simon & Schuster; Reissue edition 2009.

UMLAS, Judith W. The Power of Acknowledgment. IIL Publishing, New York, a division of International Institute for Learning, Inc. September 2007.

BRUCE GANDY, Dottie. 30 Days to a Happy Employee: how a Simple Program of Acknowledgment Can Build Trust & Loyalty at Work. Fireside; Original edition 2001.

STONE Douglas, PATTON Bruce, HEEN Sheila, FISHER Roger. Difficult Conversations: How to discuss what matters most. Penguin 1st edition April 2000.

CIALDINI, Robert B. Influence: The Psychology of Persuasion. Harper Paperbacks; Revised edition 2006.

DWOSKIN, Hale, The Sedona Method: Your Key to Lasting Happiness, Success, Peace and Emotional Well-Being. Sedona Press 2003.

ERICSSON,K Anders, KRAMPE Ralf, TESH-ROMER Clemens. The Role of Deliberate Practice in the Acquisition of Expert Performance.

RECOMMENDED READING

Honoring the Self: Self-Esteem and Personal Transformation by Nathaniel Branden. Bantam Books 1983.

Toward a Psychology of Being, by Abraham Maslow. Wiley 3rd edition (November 9, 1998).

Acknowledging what is: Conversations with Bert Hellinger by Bert Hellinger, Gabriele ten Hovel. Zeig, Tucker & Theisen (Sept 1999).

Quick Emotional Intelligence Activities for Busy Managers: 50 Team Exercises That Get Results in Just 15 minutes by Adele B. Lynn. Published by AMACOM (January 29, 2007).

Emotional Intelligence: 10th Anniversary edition; Why it can matter more than IQ by Daniel Goleman. Published by Bantam; 10 Anv edition (September 26, 2006).

ABOUT THE AUTHOR

Peter Anthony Gales is from Port-of-Spain, Trinidad and has over eighteen years of extensive multicultural and multi-national experience, having lived and worked in North America and Europe. His business experience also includes the Far East and the Caribbean.

Peter left the corporate world in 2005 and is now an energizing and engaging public speaker, writer, entrepreneur and visionary who believes that high technology, particularly the internet, is making possible a level of personal freedom and self-expression unprecedented in human history.

Primarily through his company MoreVida, Inc., and his philosophy of *The Practice of Your Life,* Peter Anthony helps individuals and organizations design and maintain practices to take care of business and personal concerns.

Peter lives in New York and winters in Trinidad.

Blog: www.thepracticeofyourlife.com
E-mail: pgales@thepracticeofyourlife.com
Linkedin: http://www.linkedin.com/in/peteranthonygales
Twitter: PeterGales